UNDERSTANDING YOUR PET TRAILHOUND

EMILY SAVAGE

COPYRIGHT

CONTENTS

CHAPTER TEN

FOREWORD

WRITTEN BY SUE LLOYD, OF LAKELAND TRAILHOUND WELFARE.

When Emily asked if I would write a foreword for this book, I felt very honoured, yet wondered how qualified I was to undertake such a task. It caused me to reflect on my Trailhound journey and it hit me that it was thirty years ago, in 1991, that I adopted my first hound, via the Hound Trailing Association. Then, in 1998, I heard about Peter Wilson starting the Trailhound Trust, and began to help him with fundraising, transporting, and finding homes. So, perhaps I have picked up a thing or two after all.

In those days, the vast majority of people outside of Cumbria had no idea what a Trailhound was. Nowadays, you are far more likely to be stopped by an admirer saying, "Is that a Trailhound? My friend/aunt/second cousin has one." I quite like the fact that Trailhounds are the dog world's best kept secret; perhaps a bit like being in the Millionaire or Mile High Club!

Emily has admirably captured all aspects of Trailhound life, from the history of the breed right through to present day hound trailing, as well as providing adopters with an insight into what new and sometimes hair-raising canine delights await them. How wonderful it would have been in the early days to have a comprehensive book like this one to refer to for training tips, when trying to solve some of the challenges of being owned by an irascible trailie. What is so exciting about the training guide is that Emily promotes and teaches the most up-to-date and positive reinforcement methods, which work so well with hounds.

Whatever your involvement with Trailhounds, you will find this book a little gem and a wealth of information. Every trailie home should have one (preferably kept high up on a shelf, as I know, to the detriment of one of my one-hundred-year-old books, that hounds are sometimes partial to a little nibble).

Lakeland Trailhound Welfare continues the work and vision of Peter Wilson and Eileen Robinson, and lifelong friendships are formed. What a unique breed.

Sue Lloyd

PREFACE

I'm really excited to be sharing my book with you, at last! This project has been a fascinating journey which has led me to better understand my own hounds, and I'm sure there will be something of interest for everyone, no matter what your involvement in the hound world. I have learned an enormous amount from those who have so kindly provided me with vital information, help and support, not to mention some absolutely stunning photography to illustrate my accounts.

This user-friendly guide to Trailhounds will provide the reader with ten stand-alone chapters packed full of details, enabling you to dip in and out as you please. The first half of my book is dedicated to tracing the development of the breed back to its early roots, whilst also delving into the history of hound trailing, its origins, and what the sport involves today, including training methods. The information enclosed will lead to a much deeper understanding of your pet hound and will give you much insight into their previous life. For those looking to acquire a hound, I will examine their suitability as a pet, the re-homing process and the routes available to you to do this. I will also look into the history of Lakeland Trailhound Welfare, whose volunteers work closely with the trailing community in order to find fantastic forever homes for their beloved racing hounds.

I will explore these extraordinary animals in their role as pets with a celebratory community chapter, where we will discover why the hounds are so loveable, what some of their best attributes are, as well as taking a look at a few of the entertaining adventures they have had in their pet homes (they certainly like to keep us on our toes!). In order to further demonstrate their versatility, I will also include a "Hall of Fame" chapter which describes charitable work undertaken, looks into the process of blood donations, and recognises some sporting achievements, notably an appearance at Crufts!

In addition to the Trailhound-specific information, the second half of the book includes chapters on what I consider to be core essentials in understanding the emotions which drive canine behaviour, and how we should respond to any behavioural challenges which may arise. I will offer guidance on how to introduce new equipment sensitively, and provide training tips which align with science-based, up-to-date, kind and ethical canine coaching methods. I will place emphasis on loose lead walking and recall, skills which many dog guardians attest to struggling with. Throughout, I will outline some common myths and beliefs which are perpetuated and are potentially harmful to your dog and the bond that you share. I will take a close look at reactivity and you will gain insight into how to read and interpret your hound's body language, enabling you to recognise and respond to the earliest signs of stress before it escalates.

I'm sure that most dog guardians are aware of the benefits and importance of incorporating enrichment into daily routine, but many are unsure of how to make the progression into scentwork. To this end, you will find some fascinating facts about the workings of the canine nose and you will have access to my twelve-step guide to introducing daily enrichment and scentwork, giving you and your furry friends hours of entertainment and fun, regardless of their age, breed, or physical capabilities.

Please read on to share in the joy of being a fully fledged member of the trailie fan club as we venture into new territory: the first ever foray into the trials and tribulations of life with a pet Trailhound!

ACKNOWLEDGEMENTS

Whilst carrying out my research, I came to realise how very little literature there is available on the subject of Trailhounds and the sport of hound trailing, therefore I'm extremely grateful to those I have heavily relied upon to share their knowledge and experience with me.

I must give special thanks to Jamie Lawless of the Border Hound Trailing Association, who has very generously shared his own research material with me, as well as answering thoroughly and with great patience my endless queries and questions. He has also kindly allowed me to share with you some of his extremely beautiful photography.

Helen Warrington very generously spent hours sifting through her vast collection of stunning photographs in order to send me a large selection to choose from, for which I'm most thankful.

Thank you to Sue Lloyd for writing my foreword; I'm really grateful for her kind words. Sue, along with the other trustees of Lakeland Trailhound Welfare, has been wonderful in offering support and information, and has answered a deluge of questions, enabling me to accurately portray the wonderful work that is carried out in conjunction with the hound trailing community.

I'm also very grateful to those of you that have sent me photographs and stories to include. I hope they will be a source of enjoyment and entertainment for all, forming a lovely tribute to our much-loved Trailhounds, both past and present.

A big thank you to Holly Leake BCCSDip.CanCare for kindly offering to proofread for me.

Last but not least, I would like to thank Sally Gutteridge of Canine Principles for her daily guidance, encouragement and reassurance.

I would never have even contemplated the idea of writing a book if it were not for her and the continuous, unwavering support from fellow students.

Thank you all, you are very much appreciated!

INTRODUCTION

Welcome to the wonderful world of the Trailhound! If you are lucky enough to have already been chosen by a trailie, I don't need to persuade you of the absolute joy they bring to our lives. If you are considering re-homing one but are, as yet, unfamiliar with the breed, I promise you have a real treat in store! The Trailhound is a little-known treasure that originates from very few parts of the UK and seems to be very much a hidden gem. When holidaying in Cumbria with my hounds, I have frequently been amazed by the number of people who say "ooooh, that's a big Beagle!" and have never heard of a Trailhound, including some of the locals!

I will explore the Trailhound's physical appearance, the development of the breed, the history of hound trailing, how the hounds are trained, and what trailing looks like today. For those who are looking to re-home, I will investigate how you might go about acquiring a hound, along with providing some guidance on how to transition them successfully from the fells to your sofa. Lakeland Trailhound Welfare works closely with the trailing community and I will look at the fantastic work they do, revealing the origins of the organisation, how it is staffed, and what their re-homing process involves. In order to provide you with a glimpse of what lies ahead, we will celebrate some of the hounds' sporting successes as pets, their charity work and various ventures, plus some of their misadventures!

Besides Trailhounds, another passion of mine is promoting science-based, positive reinforcement, force-free training and handling methods. I will guide you through how to choose suitable equipment, how to condition it before use, and I will provide you with lots of helpful tips on how to teach your hound to walk nicely on the lead, how to teach recall, and other useful behaviours such as hand targeting.

Since my hounds came into my life, I have studied continuously in order to better understand them and to learn how to address behavioural challenges that have arisen in a kind and ethical way. I will share with you some of what I have learned through my studies, and what I consider to be essential information that every dog guardian should have access to. I believe strongly in advocating for the fearful, anxious and reactive dogs out there; it is so difficult to appreciate fully the struggles that some dogs face until you are actually in the position of being the guardian of one, so I would like to share some insight with you in the hope of achieving a more sympathetic and thoughtful world for them.

Something I have struggled with my entire life is anxiety, a condition which not only affects humans, but our canine friends as well. It is only really since studying the workings of the canine brain that I have finally come to terms with my anxiety and fully understand why I sometimes feel the way I do. This has helped me to maintain an empathetic approach towards animals and really consider what they may be feeling, and how this drives their behaviour.

I believe it is vital that all dog guardians have at least a basic understanding of body language and are able to recognise the early signs of stress in order to prevent it from escalating. I will look into the experiences and insight that Mark and Spencer have gained from re-homing the lovely Suzie, whom we have all come to know and love through progress updates via the *Trailhound Appreciation Society* Facebook page. Suzie is renowned for her passion for pizza and will forever be "Suzie the pizza hound" when I think of her.

One of the challenges I have encountered as a dog guardian is reactivity, something which is widely misunderstood. Until you actually have a dog that struggles with certain things in their environment, whether that is strangers, unknown dogs, other animals, fast-moving vehicles, etc, you may never have even come across the term before. It is so easy to dismiss unwanted behaviour as naughtiness or stubbornness when, in fact, the dog is simply trying to communicate that, in that moment, he is struggling to cope and needs space. I will look at reactive behaviour in some depth to raise awareness of what it is, what it looks like, why it happens and what you can do to help your dog in terms of managing the environment, minimising exposure to triggers, and kind, ethical training to help change your dog's emotional response to the things that worry them.

The dog training world is rife with poor, outdated advice. It's a sad but true fact which can make it extremely difficult to discern who will provide science-backed, safe, Best Practice guidance; this is further complicated by the lack of regulation amongst professionals. Anyone can call themselves a dog trainer. Let's just consider the implications of this for a moment; no accreditation nor formal training necessary, no requirement to continue professional development for the duration of their working life, no regulation of their practices or methodologies. This means that selecting a professional is an absolute minefield. However, I will discuss some of the outdated theories which are sadly perpetuated, and I will provide you with the information that you need to arm yourself against the many pitfalls.

I cannot write a book about Trailhounds and not talk about their amazing sense of smell! The canine nose is absolutely fascinating. They have up to 300 million scent receptors in their nose, compared with our approximate six million which, according to Dr Michael T. Nappier DVM, DABVP of the Virginia-Maryland College of Veterinary Medicine, enables a dog to detect the equivalent of half a teaspoon of sugar in an Olympic-sized swimming pool! The canine area of the brain which processes scent is around 40 times larger than our own, which equates to a sense of smell 10,000 to 100,000 times more powerful. To help this to compute fully, James Walker, former director of the Sensory Research Institute at Florida State University, describes this in terms of sight: "If you make the analogy of vision, what you and I can see at a third of a mile, a dog could see more than 3,000 miles away and still see as well." Phenomenal! They can also use their nostrils independently, creating a 3D scent picture that allows them to pinpoint exactly where a smell originates from.

The musicians amongst you will be thoroughly impressed that dogs can also circular breathe, drawing in and processing scent at the same time as they breathe in and out, creating a constant stream of air effortlessly. Mind-blowing stuff! I will discuss the mechanics of the nose and look at ways we can incorporate enrichment and scentwork into our hounds' daily lives. Taking Scentwork UK and Mantrailing UK lessons has made an enormous difference to my nervous hound; it is helping to build his confidence and resilience, as well as being hugely enjoyable for him, while learning new skills in a higher distraction environment, around new humans and dogs. Jack wags his tail so much while we are at lessons or out trailing that I worry he is going to wear it out or it will drop off! Scentwork is suitable for dogs of any age, any physical capability, even those convalescing. Therefore, I have written a training plan tailored to suit dogs of any ability or confidence level, to provide you and your hound with hours of entertainment whilst utilising their biggest asset: their shnozz!

With this book I hope to provide you with some essential information, along with some humour, that will benefit both current and prospective Trailhound guardians. This book is also a celebration of the Trailhound, and I hope to convey what they mean to the humans that share their lives with them and the lengths that they will go to in order to cater to their hound's every whim! Once someone has had the pleasure of being owned by one hound, the second (or third…. or fourth…..) usually follows fairly swiftly! I cannot imagine life without mine now, despite the trials and tribulations of trailie guardianship: whiskers in your face and nose pressed to yours at 5:30 AM, providing you with your very own trailie alarm: "it's breakfast time human, feed me now!" wake-up call; all of your clothes/towels/dressing gowns/underwear become repurposed as trailie snuffle mats; when you're ready to climb into bed at night and you realise that you've been beaten to it and have your very own furry bed warmer all ready and waiting for you, particularly when you have only just changed the bedding. Similarly, any middle-of-the-night traipses along to the loo in a bleary, brain-fogged, sleepy haze end in confusion, mystery and puzzlement as you try to negotiate reclaiming an edge of the bed but don't want to disturb the hound, much to your other half's annoyance as you wake them up whilst fussing over the dog to make sure that they are comfortable enough. Oh, and not forgetting the eyes that will bore right into the centre of your brain from across the room while you are eating and then suddenly, as if they have apparated like a character from a Harry Potter book, you've got a snout tucked under your armpit, with a large pair of nostrils attempting to vacuum up and inhale the entire contents of your plate.

These are just a few of the many delights that trailies will brighten your life with, and I'm sure that you will become just as smitten as I have; it's impossible not to fall for their many and varied charms. They are all so individual, as all dogs are, but there is something so very special about them. As we explore the breed and read of the many unique characters and the adventures that they have shared with their humans over the years, I know you will fall head over heels for these hounds, as I have.

Photograph overleaf by Jamie Lawless of Field&Fell Photography

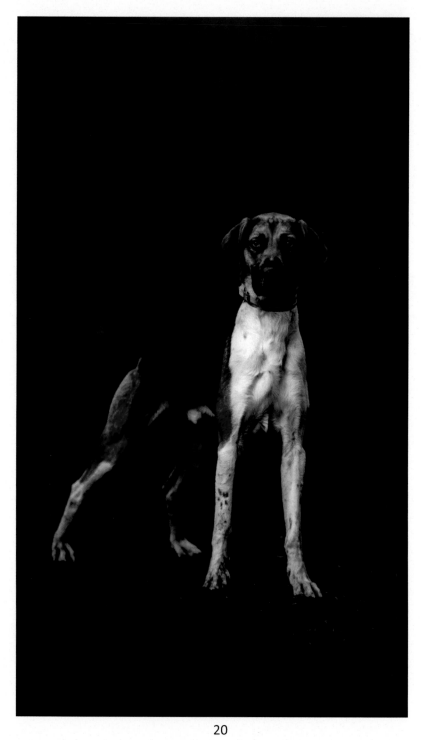

CHAPTER ONE

WHAT IS A TRAILHOUND?

Trailhounds are born and bred for the sole purpose of racing, and only those hounds with the parentage of two Trailhounds are considered to be a true Trailhound. In terms of colouring, there are many variations, including lemon, lemon and white, black, black and tan, tri-coloured (black, white and tan), black and white, and so on, but any colour variation is acceptable. The hounds are absolutely breath-taking, appearing to be very lean and extremely well-muscled; this is emphasised when they are freshly clipped, which is carried out in order to prevent the hounds from overheating when running. These hounds are exceedingly well cared for, with coats being provided to keep them warm when they are not racing *(See Fig.1)*. Incidentally, the first record of clipping is dated to 1905 at Cartmel, where sheep shears were used. According to John Coughlan, author of *Hound Trailing: A History of the Sport in Cumbria*, when Alfred Marr from Egremont clipped his hound Gladstone, he caused a tremendous uproar when Gladstone won his race; there were no established rules at this point, of course.

Upon seeing a Trailhound for the first time, the contrast between their physique and the average pet dog's is rather startling, but we must remember that these hounds are well-honed athletes and are the absolute pride and joy of the trailing community *(See Fig. 2&3)*. The hounds have a much lighter and smaller frame than a Foxhound, with different shaped ears. Many seem to have much longer toes, more akin to a sighthound than the rounded, neat feet of the Foxhound. They are built for stamina, speed and endurance, and are carefully bred for performance. Hound Trailing Association hounds are descended mainly from the Harrier, namely the Brampton Harrier, and there is also some Bloodhound to be found from the Holme Harriers line. They are founded on the Fell Hound and local Harrier blood, but the breed has developed into a type with a distinct look that is easily recognised, and has been so, for one hundred years or more. Some experimental breeding occurred when a Pointer-Harrier cross was introduced in the mid-1920s and later, in the 1950s, there was a Greyhound/Irish Setter cross; in 1962, a couple of Kerry Beagles were also tried.

Although there are puppy shows held within the associations, it is generally believed that a Trailhound should not be a show dog and it is more beneficial for the Trailhound not to have to conform to an imposed breed standard. This means that owners can select hounds and breed according to personal preference in terms of build, weight and colouring, etc *(See Fig.4&5)*.

Generally speaking, most hound trailers would prefer that the Kennel Club do not recognise Trailhounds as a breed because if it were to raise their popularity amongst the general public, it could lead to a decline in the very careful breeding that has been maintained for over two centuries. In order to safeguard against this, the hounds are neutered prior to being re-homed and puppies only become available for sale outside of the sport under very specific circumstances, such as if they are born out of season or if there is an accidental litter. Hounds are usually left intact while they are racing, as long as there are no underlying medical conditions which require them to be neutered, because it means that there is the option of breeding from them at a later date if they prove to be successful racers. It also means that they can fully mature both physically and mentally, with none of the risks associated with neutering too early. Possible issues include joint disorders such as hip dysplasia and patellar luxation, delayed closure of growth plates due to insufficient growth hormones, a higher prevalence of cranial cruciate ligament rupture, and it can also render them more susceptible to some cancers, hypothyroidism and pancreatitis.

Having two male hounds myself, I was curious to know if there was a particular preference when choosing hounds and whether there was a trend in one sex being typically more successful than the other. I'm told that any preference for having a dog or a bitch is entirely down to the owner and that some only keep bitches, whilst others have only dogs; some keep both. Bitches tend to mature quicker, especially as some dogs are comparatively large. Some owners may prefer bitches due to them usually being smaller and, interestingly, bitches are thought to be, on the whole, more consistent racers.

Most racing hounds are kennelled, so puppies would usually be whelped and raised in kennels also, unless there was a particular issue: for example, when a pup is struggling or isn't able to feed sufficiently, they may be brought into the home to be hand-fed. Unlike Foxhounds, Trailhounds do not tend to have puppy walkers but instead, puppies are kept until they are due to begin their training, with some being retained in order to be "set off" so that they can be sold once their training is in place. (I explain "setting off" more fully later on when we discuss training methods, but briefly, it refers to the period at the end of the season when the pups are between the ages of six and nine months. This time provides them with several months to learn the ropes before the trial trails begin in March or pre-season practice trails start, and it is during this time that the pups are first introduced to the trailing scent). This caters well for some of the older members of the racing community, who may no longer be able to train a hound and would prefer to buy a puppy which is race-ready. Most owners would usually train their own hounds, but there was a time when many trainers would only train other hounds. Some may take on multiple pups to train, and might either then sell them, or have an existing arrangement in place with someone to train a pup for them alongside their own. Pups are usually only socialised with their own litter or any other dogs and hounds which may be on the premises, although many bring pups to trails so that they can watch to see what goes on, and meet other people and hounds *(See Fig.6)*.

Ear tattooing is carried out at six weeks of age. The Border trailers don't tend to have their puppies' dew claws removed, while the HTA often carry out removal at around three days old. If pups aren't registered, they cannot run for the season; this will need to be done at the start of the following year. The pups' parents also need to be registered with an association, therefore pups from unknown circumstances also cannot run. However, because of COVID-19, there were a few instances last year of litters not being tattooed because it was not possible to receive someone in the trailers' homes to do this. In these rather unusual circumstances, hounds are given identity sheets which describe their markings in order to identify them, but this is a very rare occurrence.

SUITABILITY FOR RE-HOMING.

Trailhounds make absolutely wonderful pets and will soon become a fully fledged member of the family. They are extremely affectionate, playful and fun-loving and they like company, both that of family members and other household pets *(See Fig. 7)*. When re-homing any dog, they will always need to be taught how to be comfortable spending time alone, and this may take some time. You will need to commit to this while they are settling in, to avoid any separation related problems occurring. Hounds do like to be with you and involved in everything, often checking on what everyone is doing. One of mine is extremely inquisitive and if I pay a visit to the bathroom, I can guarantee that a pair of twitching nostrils and a set of whiskers will soon appear at the door, peering around the corner to see whether he is missing out on anything. You will never be lonely or have to endure solo trips to the loo again, that's for sure!

The experience of being re-homed is a big upheaval for the hounds, but they also have to transition from living in kennels in a rural part of the UK to living in a house, sometimes in more urban environments. They need to be given time to settle in, with most adapting fairly quickly to indoor life; they will be ensconced on your sofa and on your bed before you know it! Do bear in mind that a hound coming from a kennelled environment may not be toilet trained. This also applies to dogs which have previously been house-trained but have perhaps spent time in a re-homing centre.

Any dog that you take on, regardless of breed, age, circumstances etc will not know where they can go to the toilet in their new home, so will need to be trained (I will discuss this in more detail later in the book). However, Trailhounds learn quickly and are generally very clean.

The racing hounds are often driven long distances to reach some of the more remote trails, so are normally quite used to vehicles and travelling. Although some hounds are larger than others, they all seem to fit quite nicely on the back seat (safely and legally contained, of course). Trailhounds are extremely versatile and will enjoy going out on adventures with you. Some have travelled abroad and had a lovely time with their families; sunning themselves, paddling, splashing around and digging holes on the beach! *(See Fig.8&9)*. Many hounds also go on to excel at other sports, with canicross, bikejor, agility, scootering, scent detection and mantrailing being popular.

Those moving to urban areas will possibly experience heavy traffic and unfamiliar noises for the first time and will have no road sense. The hounds will have received little or no training other than their racing training, so you will need to dedicate time to work on recall and loose lead walking as a minimum requirement; it is your responsibility as a caring and responsible guardian to keep them safe at all times.

Trailhounds will require a thoroughly secured home environment as they are nose-driven scenthounds that are trained to trail independently for miles over all terrains and obstacles; the average-height garden fence will not contain them *(See Fig.10)*.

WHY MIGHT A TRAILHOUND NEED RE-HOMING?

There are several scenarios which might lead to a Trailhound being re-homed:

- Hound trailing is a very competitive sport and the rules are strict. Occasionally there will be incidents where a hound might prefer to play with or affect the performance of another hound in some way during the race, which can result in a racing ban.
- Although the hounds are always carefully bred from other racing hounds, this doesn't automatically guarantee that future puppies will take to racing; some are not well-suited to it, while others may show little interest in trailing.
- A hound might sustain a slight injury which prevents them from continuing to race because of the physical demands on the body, but can be successfully and happily re-homed as a pet.
- The hounds finish their racing career at around the age of six or seven, when they are classed as a racing veteran, but they still have a long life left to live, many reaching the grand old age of fifteen or sixteen years old.
- There are rare occasions when puppies are born outside of the racing season or an accidental litter might occur; in both cases, re-homing is required.

THE HISTORY OF TRAILING

Hound trailing takes place in only a few regions of the British Isles, being popular in Cumbria, the Scottish Borders, and parts of Yorkshire and Ireland. Its origins date back to the seventeenth century, when hunt masters arranged matches against other packs to test the speed and endurance of their own Foxhounds. At this time, King Charles II established horse racing at Newmarket, one of the world's great racing centres, with programmes for local meetings being published in the *London Gazette*. In the issue dated April 14th 1681, it stated that "There will be also a Plate given for Hounds running a Trail-scent (drag) of four Miles, for which any Gentleman may put in a hound." The following year, an issue dated April 10th 1682 announced a "Trail Scent for Hounds" and in the issue from August 21st 1684, it was reported that there would be "two Plates run for hounds the Four Miles Course, the one of 10 pound, the (other) of 5 pound price," while the issue from August 19th 1686 simply said, "There will be a Dog-Plate Run for each day".

The hounds of the 1680s were either Stag Hounds or Harriers, as foxhunting with a pack of hounds was really only just beginning at this time. Later, Hugo Meynell, the second Master (1753-1800) of the Quorn Hunt, was establishing Leicestershire as the most fashionable area to hunt in when the speed of the hounds became of greater interest. The Hon. J. H. Smith-Barry, founder and Master (1763-1784) of the Cheshire Hunt, provided the opposition. In his *Correct Delineation of the Horse and Dog* (London, 1820) John Scott wrote: "Mrs. Meynell matched two Fox Hounds, Richmond and a Bitch (his daughter Rarity) against Mr Barry's two hounds, Bluecap and Wanton, to run over the Beacon Course at Newmarket, for five hundred guineas". Mr Barry's hounds were trained by Will Crane on Tiptree Heath, Essex, where races were held annually for small prizes. Will Crane was well known in the area as a huntsman, who kept the inn at Rivenhall. His training methods comprised running a fox drag of eight or ten miles on turf three times a week over the course of two months, feeding the hounds oatmeal, milk and sheep's trotters. While Mr Meynell's hounds were training, they were fed entirely on legs of mutton and were also in excellent condition; the starting odds were seven to four. The match was held on the 30th September 1773 by laying the accustomed drag from the Rubbing House at Newmarket Town end to the Rubbing House at the starting post of the Beacon Course, with the four hounds being immediately laid on the scent. Mr Barry's Bluecap won and his hound Wanton came in a very close second, both completing the four-mile race in just seconds over eight minutes. The time is comparable to that of an ordinary "Country plate" horse carrying between eight stones and eight stones, seven pounds. Mr Meynell's hound lost by around one hundred and twenty yards, whilst the bitch didn't complete the course. Interestingly, sixty horsemen started with the hounds, but only twelve of those finished with them, with Will Crane riding the twelfth horse.

In the 1790s, Colonel Thornton of Thornville Royal in Yorkshire owned a hound bitch named Merkin, and he challenged any hound of her age in England to a five-mile race for ten thousand guineas; Merkin had previously completed a Newmarket four-mile trail in seven minutes and half a second. It was reported that Merkin's speed was still superior; she was sold in 1795 for "four Hogsheads of Claret, and the seller to have two couple of her Whelps". Later, Colonel Thornton decided to try to beat Bluecap's record. It was reported in the *Rural Sports* (London 1801) by Rev. W.B. Daniel that at two years old, Madcap was to challenge any hound in the rest of England for the price of five hundred guineas. Madcap's brother Lounger was challenged, at four years old, to a match against Hugo Meynell's Pillager, plus any other hound of his that he liked. However, Lounger was seen racing at Tattersall's, and so Meynell thought better of the challenge and forfeited the match, which had seen a bet made for two hundred guineas.

HOUND TRAILING TODAY

Hound trailing is one of the oldest sports in the Lake District. The Hound Trailing Association was formed in 1906 under the directorship of Robert Jefferson of Springfield, near Whitehaven, with the first rule book being produced in 1913. Today there is very little prize money involved in the sport, although I'm told that there was a time when winning a trail or two could exceed the wage of five days spent working down the mine! Betting is a popular part of hound trailing, and those involved in racing raise a lot of money for charity. The HTA runs the sport in the Lakes, whilst the Border Hound Trailing Association governs racing in the borders; trailing also occurs in Yorkshire and Ireland. The associations come together to race once a year, known as an International, with the hosting alternating on a yearly basis between the HTA and the BHTA.

Hound trailing involves laying a scent trail of an aniseed and paraffin mix by dragging a scent-soaked rag over a distance, usually between eight and ten miles, over fields and fells. Two trail layers start in the middle of the trail and drag the scent outwards, with one finishing at the "slip" (start) and the other going to the finish. Trails are divided into various categories: for example, there are Maiden races for those that have never won an open championship trail; Open trails, which contribute towards the championship; Produce races for the puppies, and Open Restricted races for any hounds to have won less than three open championship trails. The hounds cover the ground in around thirty minutes, but usually between twenty-five and forty, depending on the terrain *(See Fig.11)*. In the event of a hound finishing outside of these times, the trail is declared void.

Rather than following the hounds, spectators watch from vantage points, which means that the hounds are often out of sight or appear as mere specks on the fellside, making a good pair of binoculars an essential accessory! *(See Fig.12)*. If you don't mind a bit of a walk, you might be lucky enough to reach one of the road crossing points where the hounds are chaperoned safely across from one field to another, wowing you with their agility and speed.

To someone unaware of the sport, a trail event might even go unnoticed; a passer-by might see a group of cars seemingly abandoned in a field on a remote fellside and think no more of it. Upon further investigation, the hounds may be seen as they are walked on-lead to warm up, giving them plenty of opportunity to go to the toilet prior to racing, in order to make them comfortable and avoid any unnecessary stops mid-run. When it is time for their trail, they are walked to the "slip" where they assemble with lots of other hounds and their handlers *(See Fig.13)*. There is often an enormous amount of noise, as the hounds are extremely vocal and impatient to run! I can safely say that I have heard nothing quite like the sounds which emanate from these hounds when they are preparing to race; pure excitement is an understatement!

When they are waiting to be "slipped," the hounds have their coats and collars removed as the judge marks them all with a pen, ensuring that the hounds which start the race are the ones that finish. Some owners also choose to dye patches on their own hounds in order to identify them when they are racing. The hounds are held by the scruff until the starter person or incoming trail layer crosses the line *(See Fig. 14)*. There is a real risk of the hounds colliding with the starter person, which is why the hounds should not be released until he has walked through them.

As there are multiple classes for the hounds to run in, only the first longer trail for the hounds and the first shorter trail that is laid for the pups and veterans will be started by the trail layer; they will follow what is known as a "live rag" (fresh scent). For subsequent races, the hounds will follow a scent trail which has been contaminated by the previous runners, therefore it is called a "dead rag". These races are started by someone mimicking the return of the trail layer, walking ten to twenty yards out into the field and then returning to cross the starting line. The hounds usually disappear from sight rapidly, so it is then a case of watching and waiting for them to eventually come into view again, at which point the trailers begin to congregate at the finish.

When the first hounds are nearing the end, they are called in with whistles and shouts of encouragement, and as they cross the finish line, the trailers deftly slip collars back on as their hounds eagerly put their noses straight into their well-earned bowl of bait; coats are then replaced to prevent the hounds from getting cold. Once they have finished eating their bait, the hounds are walked back to the car parking area, allowing them to cool down safely on the way. Next, they are washed and dried off whilst being thoroughly checked over to ensure that they have no injuries.

The food used as bait varies from person to person but it is usually things like tripe, tinned meat, soaked biscuits, rice, pasta, chicken and fish. The hounds either have a drink with the bait, or it may be mixed in with the food to moisten it *(See Fig 15)*. Most hounds are fed once a day, but when racing, they will have the bait and then their tea once they arrive home; amazingly, they can lose up to three pounds in weight during a race! The hounds might have raw egg mixed with water, toast, or similar, as a small breakfast before racing. I've always been fascinated that some hounds are fed milky, cold tea afterwards and I'm told that this is a long-standing

31

tradition which has been passed down through the generations. There doesn't seem to be any scientific reasoning behind it, but the hounds certainly love it. Every trailer develops their own methods and preferences within the traditions of the sport in the quest to gain the winning edge!

The following photograph is of hound champion Progress with two of his three co-owners, Geoff Waite and Norman Pattinson; the third, not shown in the picture, was J. Rickerby. Progress, known as Ricky, won four Senior Championship titles, three Langholm Common Riding wins, the BHTA's biggest and most challenging trail, as well as having an international win. In four seasons he ran two hundred and eighty trails, finishing amongst the first six hounds two hundred and thirty-three times, with two hundred and two of those being in the first three. What a hound!

Photograph by kind permission of Annabelle Connelly and Jamie Lawless

TRAINING

Trailhounds begin their training very young, but the exact age will vary slightly, depending on the trainer. It usually begins with "ratching," which means that the pups are simply taken out to "hunt" around, explore and investigate, using their noses. Again, the next step also depends on the owner/trainer, but most would go on to run point to point next, known as "straight outs". This training exercise requires two people: one person holds the pup, the other walks away a short distance in a straight line, and the pup runs to them. The aim of this is twofold: first, it acclimatises the pup to being handled and held by the scruff, and second, it encourages the pup to want to run towards and find the trainer, which results in lots of praise. Once the pups are progressing well, it is time to introduce the scent to them, again via "straight outs". The distance is kept short initially and increased gradually, until the pup is able to run in a straight line, following the scent for a fair distance. He is then rewarded with "bait," a small amount of food in a bowl. The purpose of this is to create a positive association between the scent and the food reward through classical conditioning (Pavlov in action!). Some trailers place the bait bowl on the scent rag at the end, to help consolidate the scent imprinting process.

The next stage in training is to "set them off," which usually falls at the end of the season, in October, when they are between the ages of six and nine months. This allows them several months to learn the ropes before the trial trails begin or pre-season practice trails start, in March. This also means that they benefit from a month or so of practice before the winter sets in and the ground becomes too hard to run on.

Once "straight outs" are easily achieved, the next step is to add a bend or a corner to the trail. This will probably be around a dyke or hedgerow, so that the trainer won't be visible to the pup. Whilst walking away, it's best to shout and call the pup, because it will encourage them to follow once they've been "slipped". The aim of this exercise is to show the pup's willingness to venture away from the "slipper" and out of sight to find the owner.

Once the pup is able to negotiate corners with confidence, a few obstacles may be added, such as having to tackle going underneath gates, through gateways and holes in hedgerows, and so on. Jamie Lawless, of the BHTA, kindly explained to me that he has a couple of local trails of varying lengths which he uses: one about three minutes long and the other approximately four to five minutes long. He describes one of these as a small loop, a three-minute trail crossing seven fields, including gateways and going under a fence. This loop is tackled in three stages, and when the pup can complete each of those, the next stage in the progression is to run a looped trail. Depending on the land the trailers have permission to use, this may be a circuit of one large field, or the loop may go through gateways leading into multiple fields. At this point, it is likely that two people will still be needed, as the pup will expect to find the owner with the reward. Once the pup feels confident though, it may be possible to lay the trail without the pup seeing the owner walking away from them, and then "slip" the pup with others.

Jamie stresses the importance of varying the trail, obstacles and location whilst training, to ensure that the hounds do indeed follow the scent and do not simply commit a trail to memory; they must remain keen to run and stay on the scent trail, with the trainer taking care that the pups do not become disinterested through repetition. They will eventually remember the practice trail routes as they become more familiar, but in the early days at least, sessions need to remain as randomised as possible.

Some trailers will train pups together, whilst others prefer to train them independently; it is vital that the pups can run without relying on having others to follow. However, it may be helpful for a pup to have guidance from a more experienced hound, which is why owners will sometimes place an older hound with pups to guide them around a trail if they are struggling. Difficulties may present in many forms: some pups may be playful on the slip and need encouragement to trail, in which case one would use a competent pup or hound to give them a lead. Some may struggle when encountering obstacles such as hedges, fences or gates which need to be jumped, so following a more experienced hound will be hugely beneficial to help them build confidence and improve. The aim is to have the pups running confidently with others over a trail that is a few minutes in length by the time that the pre-season trails start.

Trailers refer to the races in duration rather than distance, choosing suitable venues for their pups according to the time taken to complete a trail. Because of the varied terrain that is covered, the distance does not reflect the difficulty of the trail, therefore going by time allows for a more graduated approach to increasing endurance. Every trail is timed, with the stop watch being stopped when the first hound crosses the finish line. If a hound comes in earlier than the expected time, it is clear that he has not completed the trail and has deviated from the scent. Fixtures are advertised and listed by how many minutes the trails take to complete; the distance does not feature at all. The trails will progress from three minutes to six or seven minutes long by the time of the pre-season trails, which are official practices open to the whole association. These help the pups to gain further experience and build fitness for the coming season, with the aim of being able to run a trail of at least ten minutes by the time that official trial trails commence.

Most young hounds going into their pup season are around eleven to thirteen months old when they begin their careers, and standard pup trails are around five to seven miles long, with adult hounds running seven to ten miles, depending on the venue. Once the pup season has finished, they are classed as senior hounds, affectionately known as "old dogs" amongst the trailers. Hounds are classed as veterans at six years of age, and the category that is open to six-year-olds and upwards will become available to them, although they can still run with the younger hounds. The BHTA categories include: Hounds, Maidens, Pups, Pup Maidens, Graded, Restricted Graded, Open Maidens, Veterans, and All In.

Photography provided with kind permission from Jamie Lawless of Field&Fell Photography, and Helen Warrington.

Fig.1 Photograph by Jamie Lawless of Field&Fell Photography

Fig.2 Photograph by Jamie Lawless of Field&Fell Photography

Fig.3 Photograph by Helen Warrington

Fig.4 Photograph by Helen Warrington

Fig.5 Photograph by Jamie Lawless of Field&Fell Photography

Fig.6 Photograph by Helen Warrington

Fig.7 Photograph by Helen Warrington

Fig.8 Photograph by Helen Warrington

Fig.9 Photograph by Helen Warrington

Fig.10 Photograph by Helen Warrington

Fig.11 Photograph by Helen Warrington

Fig.12 Photograph by Helen Warrington

Fig.13 Photograph by Helen Warrington

Fig.14 Photograph by Helen Warrington

Fig.15 Photograph by Helen Warrington

Photograph by Helen Warrington

Photograph by Helen Warrington

"The Slip," by Jamie Lawless of Field&Fell Photography

Photograph by Jamie Lawless of Field&Fell Photography

CHAPTER TWO

LAKELAND TRAILHOUND WELFARE

In 1997, Peter Wilson set up the Lakeland Trailhound Trust from his home in Bewaldeth to promote Trailhounds as pets and to find homes for them when they retired from racing in the Lake District. Peter had a variety of rescue breeds, which he enjoyed taking to Crossbreed and Mongrel Club shows in the mid-1990s. When Peter heard of a Trailhound named Jinny who needed a home, this marked the start of his love affair with the breed. Sadly, no records exist from those earlier days of LTT, but Peter slowly built a relationship with the trailing community, locally advertising the hounds and privately re-homing through careful selection. With a small group of helpers, they were able to develop contacts with reputable animal welfare charities who took hounds in on behalf of LTT, as there were more hounds needing homes than the small organisation could adopt out in those days.

The LTT team developed a website and attended fundraising events and shows in order to further promote the breed across the country, including at Crufts. Peter attended the show in 2002 when one of his hounds, Mandy, won PRO Dogs Pet of the Year and in 2005, Mandy was nominated for a Hero of the Year award at Crufts after she raised the alarm when a fire broke out in Peter's farmhouse. Lady, a resident at the Lakeland Trailhound Trust kennels for many years, won the Grand Final for bitches in the Companion Dog Club competition at London's top canine event Discover Dogs in 2006. Lady has been a Pets As Therapy dog for many years, along with several of Peter's dogs. Peter worked tirelessly, taking in hounds right until his retirement.

Peter with Lady

In 1998, Eileen Robinson and Sue Lloyd became involved with the Lakeland Trailhound Trust. Eileen's husband Keith had racing hounds, so her role was very much pivotal. Eileen knew the trailing community well, gaining their trust and confidence, and she became the coordinator for re-homing and placing hounds, building up contacts with a number of re-homing centres throughout the country. Eileen spent many hours a day on the telephone discussing hounds; she was very passionate and inspired many others to become involved in re-homing Trailhounds.

Photograph from 2014 of Eileen (left) with Susan Purdon, Zach and Pandy

Sue Lloyd acquired her first hound in 1991 by contacting the Hound Trailing Association directly, as there was no re-homing provision at that time. Margaret Baxter, the secretary of the HTA, was the lady responsible for matching Sue with Koshka. Sue later offered to help Peter with fundraising and finding homes; she has a letter dated from 1998 that she received from him in response to her offer. This contact brought about Sue's first visit to Cumbria that same year to meet Peter, with Koshka going along with her to collect a hound due to be re-homed in Malvern. Koshka used to accompany Sue to work at a day centre for adults with learning disabilities and was very popular!

Barbara and Martin Leopold gained their first hound, who was called Stripe, in 1997. He was actually a Collie cross (or Trollie!), the result of an accidental farmyard "meeting," yet they were often asked what his racing name was! Barbara and Martin visited Peter's kennels in 2006 to adopt another hound but, due to a myriad of reasons, it wasn't until 2009 that they finally acquired another Trailhound. As Martin and Barbara were travelling up and down the M6 regularly, Eileen took advantage of their offer to transport Trailhounds to Dogs Trust centres in Harefield and Canterbury, and for private re-homings. Since then, Barbara has continued to do this, carrying out home checks and fostering many hounds and pups. Barbara has transported almost two hundred hounds for re-homing in the last eleven to twelve years, and has a particular interest in the bloodlines and breeding of Trailhounds. Barbara has been keeping records over the last ten years or so, and frequently draws up family trees for re-homed hounds. Wherever possible, she tries to connect families together who have hound siblings. Barbara's record keeping and anecdotal evidence suggests that there may be a genetic predisposition to splenic tumours, heart murmurs and thyroid issues. Three of her own hounds are regular blood donors at the Royal Veterinary College, but more on this later.

When Peter retired in 2007, the decision was made to change the name of Lakeland Trailhound Trust to Lakeland Trailhound Welfare. Eileen discussed the name replacement with one of the HTA executive members and felt that "Lakeland Trailhound Welfare" better reflected the work that they were doing. At this time, they were also not technically a "trust"; Eileen ran things so efficiently that nothing was ever formalised. In January 2015, when

Eileen sadly retired because of ill health, trustees were appointed and Lakeland Trailhound Welfare became an unregistered charity with a formal trust deed. Due to being such a small organisation, insufficient income was being generated to warrant the registration. Lakeland Trailhound Welfare is the only organisation in the country solely dedicated to re-homing Trailhounds.

Barbara Leopold very kindly sent me the first official write-up and advert for Lakeland Trailhound Trust, which both appeared in the HTA annual of 2004; the article will be of particular interest to those who, like me, live in Norfolk. I'm told by Grant Long, the original founder of *Norfolk Trailhounds*, that when the club was active, there were over two hundred members! I knew nothing of this connection when I created the Facebook page *Norfolk Unofficial Trailhounds Group* in 2015, so it is wonderful to know that we have rekindled something very special in continuing the connection between the Lakes and Norfolk.

The following is a transcription of Eileen's write-up:

The Trailhound Trust

Contributed by Eileen Robinson.

"The Trailhound Trust in now in its 6th year, and during that time has successfully re-homed over 400 trailhounds as pets. They have been re-homed in areas such as Lincolnshire, Worcestershire, Nottingham and Norfolk. Each hound that comes into the Trust is assessed by Peter, and its needs are catered for until a vacancy occurs at one of the re-homing centres with which we deal.

When kennels become available I then arrange transport, and usually 4 or 5 hounds travel together. When they arrive at the centre they are assessed as to their particular needs, and during the week they are spayed or neutered and then micro-chipped. They are then put up for adoption to new homes. This means that the centre has full control during every hound's life, and if a problem occurs, they can re-take in any hound at any time. This does not happen very often because the hounds are very adaptable and most settle into their new way of life easily.

We at the Trust keep in touch with the progress of the re-homing, both with the centre and the new owners, and our telephone numbers are available at all times, so we know exactly how each hound is progressing during its new home life.

I recently stayed in Norfolk for a week and visited several hounds in their new homes, and I am pleased to report that they were all very happy and have adjusted very well. Norfolk is a very rural area and a lot of the hounds have been re-homed with people who have horses, and so the hounds have the benefit of living in the home as a pet but also have several acres to run around in. The people in Norfolk love their hounds so much that they have formed their own Hound Club where they meet every month to discuss the delights of owning a trailhound as a pet, and the hounds are often seen at local horse shows where they enjoy the attention.

A great deal of unforseen (sic) work goes into running the Trust, not to mention expense. Apart from the odd donation, it is funded by Peter out of his pension. Transport costs, feeding, vet bills and administration all have to be paid for. Please help to support the Trust in any way you can, because without it a lot of these hounds would not be enjoying the life they have today; and for the future of hound trailing in to-day's climate we must be concerned about the welfare of the hounds. If we can demonstrate this, it will help to attract young people into the sport and will satisfy public concern about the future of hounds which do not make the grade as competitors."

THE LAKELAND TRAILHOUND TRUST

HOME FOR RETIRED TRAILHOUNDS

H.T.A. Approved

P.A.T. and HOSPITAL VISITING DOGS

&

CHARITY FUND RAISING DOG TEAM

Scalegill Sanctuary~Bewaldeth
Cockermouth~Cumbria CA13 9SY

Today, LTW continues to operate with a team of unpaid, highly dedicated volunteers who help with all aspects of promoting and re-homing hounds. There are four trustees who oversee the running and accountability of the charity; all are very passionate about Trailhounds and also carry out their work on an unpaid basis. Barbara and Sue look after the re-homing and liaise with re-homing centres which take hounds, as well as arranging private re-homing. They primarily transport the hounds to centres themselves, with Barbara usually covering the north to south-east routes and Sue covering the north to south-west routes. These hounds usually go straight from their racing home to a re-homing centre, following an overnight stay with Barbara or Sue, who pass on as much information as they can to the staff. Barbara is also involved in trailing and has a good rapport with the trailing community. Caroline Allen is the treasurer, who has a wealth of information on such matters, and she also takes on the mammoth task of putting together the LTW calendar every year. Jenny Thomas helps with many different tasks at a moment's notice, and there are a variety of volunteers that are called upon, mainly for home visits so that potential adopters, usually outside of the Cumbria area, can meet a hound and ask questions.

LTW works closely with members of the hound trailing community to help them find good retirement homes for their hounds. They offer assistance to hounds in the Border HTA, HTA and Yorkshire HTA, re-homing many youngsters who do not take to racing, as well as older retired hounds. Although LTW is the main re-homing route, when hounds from the HTA don't make the grade, they are often re-homed with trailing people in the Borders, Yorkshire and Ireland, and many go on to have very successful careers.

To initiate the re-homing process via LTW, racing owners contact Barbara or Sue, who request as much background information as they can, including racing injuries, whether the hound has been around children and cats, and what their general demeanour is. Some owners are happy to allow LTW to decide whether a hound goes to a re-homing centre or not, while others ask for a private home to be found, which then leads to a foster placement. LTW does not have a large bank of fosterers because many trailing owners like to keep their hounds whilst a suitable home is arranged, but fosterers include Sue, Barbara, Caroline and Jenny, as well as a couple in Yorkshire. Going into a foster home first is of great benefit, as it enables the hounds to acclimatise to living in a home and it means that their temperament can be more accurately assessed over a period of time, rather than assessing during a brief visit to the racing owner's kennels; the hounds can change immensely when removed from the other hounds within the kennel environment. Some trailers wish to keep their hound with them until LTW finds a suitable home, in which case, LTW arranges for the racing owner to take the hound to the vet themselves for neutering etc, for which LTW covers the cost. Occasionally trailers will re-home their hound entirely with no external input, but LTW always offers to pay for the neutering and to help with home checks, if required.

In terms of the running costs of LTW, the overheads are generally low as all trustees, volunteers and helpers are unpaid. Trailers pay a nominal donation of around £30 when their hounds come in to LTW, while others opt to donate extra. However, a hound would never be turned away if someone could not afford to make a

58

donation. The average cost per hound that LTW meets is around £160 to £200, with the variation being due to bitch neutering costing more than castration. This price covers neutering, vaccinating, worming and flea treatments, with LTW making these arrangements.

There have been occasions when a bitch has not long finished a season, which means that the vet will not neuter for three months. If the adopter is well known and trusted, the hound can be re-homed and the neutering paid for at a later date. This costs more, with external vets charging in excess of £200 per neuter, with a certain Scottish vet charging £325 on one occasion! However, some veterinary clinics are extremely generous and kindly give LTW a charitable rate for their services. Any hound with a racing injury might occasionally require extra veterinary work, and some hounds may need further care, such as the removal of skin tags or dental work. A particular hound which came into LTW last year needed to have a big operation, and his total veterinary costs were in the region of £2,000. Other expenses include fuel and food for the hounds in foster, and on odd occasions when an elderly hound being re-homed has ongoing health issues, LTW has also covered those costs.

Since 1997, LTW has homed over fifteen hundred hounds that have retired from trailing, with approximately fifty to sixty hounds a year being placed all over the country. Sometimes adopters come to Cumbria for a weekend in order to meet their chosen hound and then return home with them. Many hounds are found placements in reputable re-homing centres which neuter, vaccinate, microchip and worm dogs before re-homing them, as LTW feels that this is the only responsible way to re-home.

When LTW places hounds privately, a questionnaire is sent out following initial contact being made, unless the adopter is already known to LTW due to having re-homed a Trailhound previously; this is a regular occurrence, as one is never enough! Prospective adopters are always encouraged to ring for a chat, as many are unfamiliar with the breed and may never have seen one before, nor have any knowledge of them; they are always urged to research the breed carefully first to ensure a suitable match. LTW provides a full history of each hound, and any which stay with Sue or Barbara will be assessed around livestock; hounds can be cat-tested if required. In terms of children, interactions that the hounds have had when with the racing owners are recorded. LTW is cautious and careful about re-homing with children, but families with children are not ruled out; assessments are always made on an individual basis and a member of LTW, usually Barbara or Sue, will visit you in your home to discuss requirements and suitability. Sometimes known, trusted people are asked to help with any enquiries in their locality. Once a suitable hound is found, meetings are arranged, although COVID-19 has interfered somewhat with this process more recently. Once everyone is in agreement and a contract has been signed, there is an adoption fee of £120 (at the time of writing) and a month's free insurance is available through PETPLAN.

Puppies rarely become available for re-homing to the general public. There may be a few that LTW homes due to being born at the wrong time of year for racing, therefore will not be tattooed or registered, and there is sometimes the odd litter an owner sells on privately. There has been a decline in the number of registered puppies to less than a hundred, due to fewer younger people coming into the sport. The LTW figures state that in 1999 there were thirty-five litters with two hundred and forty-seven Trailhound puppies born, but by 2009 this had dropped to twenty litters and one hundred and fifty-nine pups. In 2019 the numbers had further decreased to just eight litters and sixty-six pups. The HTA membership numbers have also reduced considerably since 1997, when there were seven hundred and twenty-seven members and one hundred and eighty-eight kennels; in 2009 the figures were six hundred and fifty members and one hundred and eighty kennels, and in 2016, this had dropped further to three hundred and eighty-three members and one hundred and seventeen kennels.

For many years the LTW private homing figure was around fifteen annually, with around forty-five to fifty going to re-homing centres. This has changed in the last four years or so, and they are currently homing over thirty privately. The overall number taken in maintains at around fifty to sixty, although as fewer hounds are born each year, that number may actually diminish. In 2020, LTW had an unprecedented number of enquiries to adopt. They broke another record in 2020 by privately homing thirty-two hounds, with a further eighteen going to re-homing centres. Increasingly, racing owners request that LTW privately homes for them to avoid having their hounds go to re-homing centres.

LTW is indebted to the Dogs Trust and a number of reputable shelters all over the country for enabling many great adopters to encounter Trailhounds for the first time, whom otherwise may never have even heard of the breed. Dogs Trust also kindly covers the cost of any veterinary work when the hounds go to their centres. Many of those who follow the *Trailhound Appreciation Society* Facebook page acquired their first hound from a branch of Dogs Trust or Worcestershire Animal Rescue Shelter, but then went directly to LTW for subsequent hounds. Most of the hounds which are privately homed go to people who have previously owned one and are looking for another. Currently, there are more people waiting to adopt than there are hounds available!

Many great and long-lasting friendships, both human and canine, have been formed through having a re-homed Trailhound, and Facebook groups such as the *Trailhound Appreciation Society*, *Lakeland Trailhound Welfare* and *Norfolk Unofficial Trailhounds Group* facilitate this. Numerous racing owners have become friends and stay in touch with their hounds' adoptive families, with many returning to the Lakes for summer holidays with their hound, often leading to further direct adoptions. Local get-togethers happen regularly all over the country, which is wonderful for both the hounds and their humans. They are able to share their love and enthusiasm for the breed, whilst commiserating with each other over training troubles and laughing at their hounds' idiotic escapades while they run around together, going from pocket to pocket and person to person for a treat and a fuss.

During the summer, LTW promotes Trailhounds at dog shows, and organises fund-raising events throughout the year to help cover transport costs, kennelling and vet bills. LTW actively encourages people to attend and support them, and also welcomes supporters to organise and arrange their own fundraising events. For further ideas, please visit their website and have a look at their NEWS page to read about some of the events that have been held on their behalf. LTW has merchandise for sale such as calendars, car stickers, hats and fleeces, which helps financially while providing an advertising opportunity. The hound trailing community also raises funds for LTW by donating the proceeds from some of their trails.

If anyone would like further information or is interested in becoming involved in fundraising events, please contact LTW via the website www.trailhoundwelfare.org.uk, and there is also the Facebook page, as mentioned above. Contact details are provided on both and you will also find their bank details listed on the website, if you would like to make a donation.

CHAPTER THREE

THE TRANSITION FROM KENNELS TO HOME LIFE

Besides re-homing privately or via Lakeland Trailhound Welfare, another option for locating a Trailhound to take on as a pet is to contact the re-homing centres that work alongside LTW, such as branches of the Dogs Trust and the Worcestershire Animal Rescue Shelter, in Malvern. Re-homing centres will take you through a very thorough process, which I will outline in order to prepare you for what this route of adoption might entail. The following applies to any dog that is re-homed, not specifically to Trailhounds, but I will highlight the points which are of particular importance and relevance.

RE-HOMING VIA AN ANIMAL SHELTER

When re-homing any dog through an animal shelter, the adoption advisors do all that they can to ensure an excellent match, to prevent the need arising for the dog to be re-homed again. Many checks are carried out and although it guarantees nothing, it reduces the odds of an unsuccessful match. Consideration has to be taken on both sides: the dog's breed and size, his history, any health or behavioural issues, the people's experience, lifestyle, housing situation, and family structure. Any dog to be re-homed will need an outdoor environment with adequate fencing in order to keep him safe and secure. This is extremely important, particularly so for Trailhounds, who think nothing of popping over a five-bar gate, fence or hedge. They need people who will cater to their exercise requirements and, for those previously unfamiliar with the breed, you will now have a fair idea of their physical capabilities and the range of activities they might enjoy. Everyone who will live with the dog needs to agree to taking him on and be prepared for all that it involves. If there are already resident dogs, the family will need to take responsibility for introducing the new dog carefully, often in advance and at the shelter so that their staff can oversee this and ensure a smooth transition for all.

Assessments are made on a case-by-case basis, with intake questions being used to make matches, as well as the application questions about the potential new owners. Different organisations have their own requirements and procedures for the adoption process, with some being better than others, but all follow similar guidelines. At the point of hand-over from the previous owner, they will be questioned regarding the following:

- Name
- Age
- Breed
- Sex
- Feeding schedule.
- History
- Who the dog has lived with.
- Current exercise requirements.
- Whether the dog is crate trained.
- Whether the dog has any behavioural or medical issues.
- Whether there is a history of aggression, including biting.
- Whether the dog can live with other animals.
- Whether the dog is reactive.
- Whether the dog is a resource-guarder.

Shelters will also question the potential adopter to gauge the type of dog they are looking for, and will be asked:

- What their housing situation is.
- If they have any other pets.
- If they have registered with a vet.
- Whether there are any behavioural issues they will not tolerate.

- How much time will the dog be expected to spend alone on a day-to-day basis.
- Whether any form of enrichment will be offered.

Any inaccurate information provided is detrimental to the chances of a good match. Potential adopters should also ask questions of the shelter, and should be wary if they are not asked to provide details regarding their home, or if no information about the dog is forthcoming. Even dogs that have no history should spend time with the shelter staff to enable them to get to know him and make an accurate assessment of him, so that he may be placed with the right home.

Once an application to adopt has been reviewed, there is a spoken interview which may be carried out by telephone or in person; it may even take place during the first meeting with the dog. However, this is to be avoided due to the likelihood of distraction if the dog is present. The adopter may be asked for further clarification on some points, or may be questioned on something that hasn't yet been covered. The adopter can also ask about a particular dog they would like to know more about; showing an active interest would stand them in good stead and be viewed positively by the shelter. Once there is a potential match, a meeting is arranged so that the person and dog can interact. The recommendation is to sit and relax and allow the dog the time to have a sniff and to settle. If this stage goes to plan, then the process will move to the next step, which is the home check.

The home check is an important part of the adoption process for many shelters, as it enables them to verify the location, suitability, and safety of the dog in their potential new home. Some rescues insist on a home check before they release the dog, but this can happen at various stages of the process and may be combined with the interview. Any potential issues can be identified, and it gives the shelter staff the opportunity to get to know the adopter a little better. A representative from the shelter will visit and check both the interior and exterior of the house, helping to identify and rectify any potential hazards, whilst ensuring the security of the property and its boundaries. The interior assessment includes checks such as:

- Not leaving things in reach of the dog which may be chewed.
- Security of any windows that the dog can reach.
- Any house plants or substances which might be toxic.
- No electrics are left exposed.

The exterior checks will include:

- Whether the yard or garden is suitably fenced.
- Whether there is any shelter.
- Where the dog will sleep during the day and at night.
- Whether the yard is clean.
- Whether there are any toxic plants outside.
- Whether there is any risk of digging.
- Whether any gates are kept locked.
- Whether there is a pool, and if so, is it adequately protected?
- Whether there any other pets in the home and are they healthy.
- Where the nearest veterinary practice is.

All checks focus on safety and wellbeing to give the dog the best possible chance. Once the re-homing process is completed, the adoption will be finalised after references have been checked. A trial period may be offered, and there will be paperwork to fill in; any documents will be transferred to the new owner and microchip details will be updated.

The adopters need to be prepared to commit for the lifetime of the dog and plan for the next ten to fifteen years; during this time, much could change. The dog's needs must be prioritised and the adopter must actively commit to providing nutrition, healthcare, training and shelter, freedom from discomfort, pain, injury or disease, the freedom to express normal behaviour, and keep them free from fear and distress. Learning how to read the dog's body language is essential in order to understand how he might be feeling; I will cover this in detail later in the book. The humans must be fully committed to prioritising the needs of their dog, and seeing him through any struggles or challenges.

THE HONEYMOON PERIOD

As the dog settles in and transitions from the "honeymoon period," it is possible that new behaviours may appear, some perhaps undesirable. As confidence levels increase, these behaviours may become more apparent and it may seem to the adopter that things are not going well. Awareness of the honeymoon phase and what it might entail will help the adopter maintain some perspective and not feel negatively about the dog.

Some dogs will be quite subdued when they first arrive at their new home and might appear to be quiet and well-behaved, getting along with the other household residents. The experience of a new home with new people, a new routine, and novel sights, sounds and smells can overwhelm and cause emotional shutdown and suppression of behaviours, giving the appearance that the dog is coping. As time goes by and the dog gains confidence, any new behaviours emerging may have gone undetected by the shelter, which can lead to the adopter feeling as though they have been misled. It is possible that a trigger for a particular behaviour may not have been encountered while the dog was at the shelter, because handling is usually very structured and consistent, therefore the opportunities for some behaviours to surface simply do not occur. Good re-homing centres match prospective adopters carefully, as it would be detrimental to the dog to withhold any information which could affect their placement, or compromise a successful transition into their new forever home.

From this point onwards, please note that the following guidelines cater for dogs of all temperaments and backgrounds. One of my hounds is wary of strangers and unknown dogs; he also struggles a little with novelty in the home, so I'm very much drawing on my experiences with him. I hasten to add that many hounds are extremely exuberant, absolutely love anybody and everybody and will lick you to death, whether or not you like it! I don't wish to give the impression that all hounds are nervous, only that adopters should be aware of how their new hound might be feeling and that they should be given the time and space to feel comfortable. There is a popular Facebook meme which portrays a 3-3-3 rule, outlining that it takes three days to relax a little, three weeks to settle in, and three months to be fully comfortable in their new home. Although it is helpful to a degree, it is quite prescriptive and doesn't allow for the dog's individuality, previous experiences, and genetic components at play. Each dog should be given as much time and space as they need, without feeling pressured to conform to any preconceived ideas or expectations.

BRINGING HOME YOUR NEWLY ADOPTED HOUND

When an adopter brings their new furry family member home for the first time, it can be a huge upheaval for the dog, and even more so if he is a little nervous or rather anxious. He is likely to experience a wide range of emotions, so adjusting to his new home may not be a quick process. Some dogs may settle fairly easily but it takes time, patience and understanding to build trust, while giving the dog space to feel safe. To ensure as smooth a transition as possible, the adopter needs to take things slowly and not have any expectations, except, perhaps, that the dog may be a little unsure of them and may find novel things worrying or even frightening; this particularly applies to dogs transitioning from living in kennels to living in a home. Remember that a racing hound may never have lived in a house, so noisy household appliances such as washing machines, dishwashers and vacuum cleaners may seem alien to them.

There will be lots for them to process and we must remember that they have much keener hearing than we do, with their sense of smell being many times more sensitive; therefore, we may not always be able to tell what might have startled them. If they show uncertainty around any household objects or items, they should not be actively encouraged to investigate, but should be given the space to approach or move away, if that is what they choose to do. Pairing the presence of an object of uncertainty with high-value food can really help to form a more positive association, and your dog will appreciate the option to retreat to a safe distance with something tasty and long-lasting to chew on to help him feel better.

It is important to note that pairing high-value treats with things that they find challenging does not translate as "rewarding poor behaviour"; we are purely helping the dog to form a positive conditioned emotional response through classical conditioning. This is a very important part of learning theory, which I will talk about later in more depth. I also need to clarify that it is absolutely fine to comfort your dog if he seeks contact and reassurance when feeling unsure. Despite popular belief, it is not possible to reinforce emotions, only behaviours, so do not be concerned that providing comfort will make things worse. However, if we do not respect how the dog is feeling, choosing to disregard their worries and continue to expose or attempt to lure them in the hope of helping them to overcome their fear, we can certainly compound and increase it.

A plan of what happens once the new dog arrives should be made in advance to minimise any stress for everyone involved, as well as for the dog; this includes finding and registering with a good veterinary practice. Items such as food, bowls, beds, toys, barriers, crates, cleaning products, a collar, lead and harness should have been purchased already. Before the dog arrives, the adopter should think about where he will go to the toilet and who will take him, how he will be introduced to the other householders, and to the house and garden.

Consideration needs to be given as to where he will sleep during the day, and also overnight. Having said that, where he chooses to sleep may be a little surprising, with him possibly opting for the floor (or sofa/your bed/your favourite chair) rather than a new luxury dog bed. As long as his chosen place is safe and convenient, the adopter can provide encouragement and build a positive association by rewarding any interest he shows in the bed, progressing to rewarding when he touches it, and eventually when he moves onto it. Realistically though, your hound will soon be sprawled across your bed, will have rearranged your pillows and cushions and will prefer to cosy up with his humans; a safe space for him with his own comfy bed is always welcome, however.

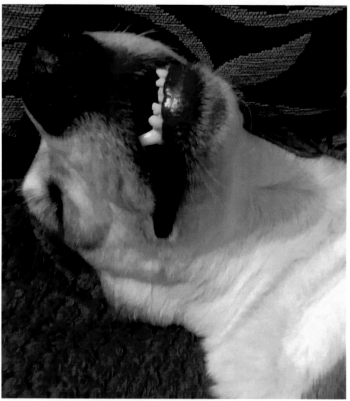

Come Home Jack making himself comfy!

If he is crate trained, will not be crated during the day and he feels safe in one, the adopter can position the crate near to them at night to help the dog feel more secure. If he isn't already crate trained, this is extremely worthwhile doing, so that he has a safe place to go when he cannot be supervised, or if he just needs a break. It is also extremely useful for when he needs to travel in the car, visit the vets and stay in their kennels, or in the case of any emergencies which may arise. As a side note, crates must never be used as a means of punishment or time-outs; they should always remain a positive and safe space for the dog, where they get pleasant things to eat and peace and quiet.

On arrival, and when the adopter is ready to take the dog indoors, he should be allowed to explore with a houseline attached (if he is comfortable wearing one) so that he can be taken outside easily and without having to make a grab for him. He should be given gentle praise as he discovers his bed, toys, bowls etc, with the adopter monitoring him while he is exploring. The household should be kept as calm as possible, with any areas that the dog should not have access to gated off so that he is set up to succeed from the outset. However, be aware that Trailhounds are extremely agile and it is unlikely that the average child safety gate will contain them. It is possible to buy extra tall ones, but anything valuable that you prefer your hound not to have access to should be put away safely. Bra fetishes soon become rather expensive, so it is better to keep doors closed, rather than have to retrieve underwear from your hound's bed that he has snaffled from the washing basket.

Always set them up to succeed; the first few days may be stressful so it is important to be prepared, plan ahead, and be consistent. Any fencing and entrance/exit points around the property should be examined to ensure that they are secure and tall enough to safeguard against escape attempts, and the dog should be supervised to keep him safe and sound. If the dog will be able to see beyond the boundaries to things which might worry him, then installing some privacy screening would also be beneficial.

Family members should sit and allow the dog to approach them if he chooses to, without attempting to restrain him in any way; any interactions should receive gentle praise. Discuss with family members the importance of softening their body language, speaking gently, and monitoring for any signs of stress. Any petting and interactions should always be the dog's choice, with frequent

71

consent checks happening. Stroke for a few seconds at a time and then stop to see how he responds; he will soon let you know if he wants more fussing!

APPROACH AVOIDANCE CONFLICT

An important point here is not to lure the dog to interact if he is at all hesitant. Attempting to lure a dog who is feeling unsure about something or someone and encouraging him to approach through coaxing and offering tasty treats can cause what is known as approach-avoidance conflict. An internal struggle can occur where the dog has to decide whether the attraction of the food outweighs his uncertainty, and he might well find himself too close and outside of his comfort zone when he approaches for the food. This may cause him to panic, and might even lead to a bite if he is very frightened. He always needs to have the option to move away and an escape route to help him feel safe.

Family and friends may want to visit straight away when you have a new addition to the family, but it is often very difficult for others to restrain themselves and take notice of requests to give the dog space when they are excited to meet the newcomer; understandably, this can be quite overwhelming for the dog. There should be no consideration of introductions to non-household members for the time-being, to allow the dog time to adjust. His needs should take precedence over friends and relatives wanting to meet the new family furbaby! If having visitors or any other disruptions in the home are unavoidable, he will need to go to his safe space with something to chew on to occupy and soothe him until the house is calm again.

TOILET TRAINING

A routine that helps him to understand when toilet and meal times are, while incorporating regular down time to rest and relax, will be really beneficial. Toilet accidents might still happen, even if the dog was previously toilet trained. It will take him time to learn where he can relieve himself in his new environment, so a good enzymatic cleaner is a must. It works by crystallising the urine and diffusing the smell, which will also help to reduce the chance of further mishaps in the same place. Puppy pads are useful if the dog is not keen on going outdoors to toilet; some consideration of the surface that he is expected to toilet on is also necessary. Dogs that have been kennelled will often have eaten, slept and toileted in the same area, so it is unfair to place unrealistic expectations on them; the dog will need to be taken out to toilet after he has eaten, had a drink, or slept. If accidents happen, remain calm at all times, clean thoroughly, watch him more carefully and, above all, he should not be punished or scolded as it may frighten or confuse him and it will damage the trusting bond that will be developing. Telling him off will make him feel insecure and wary, and he will simply resort to going to the toilet when there is nobody present. If your hound does toilet in the house, take a rolled-up newspaper and bonk yourself on the head with it repeatedly while saying, "I must watch my hound more carefully and take him out to the toilet more often." The dog should be showered in treats and praise when he goes where you would like him to. If only there were a treat party every time that *we* went to the bathroom.......

Sadly, people often complain that their dog has toileted in the house to spite them and claim that he knows what he is doing because he looks guilty, but this could not be further from the truth. The "guilty looks" result from the dog feeling intimidated and worried by the response of their trusted person. According to current scientific studies, dogs have the equivalent emotional range of a two-and-a-half year old child and experience feelings which include: excitement (what we describe as arousal), distress, contentment, disgust, fear, anger, joy, suspicion and affection. The development

73

of emotions halts at this point, so their emotional range does not progress further to encompass shame, pride, guilt and contempt. It is rather sad to think that the countless videos shared on social media portraying "guilty" dogs actually only highlight the complete misunderstanding of their family, showing the dog's confusion and uncertainty; there is never an excuse for shaming or punishing animals.

While we are discussing toilet training, I must share with you a story that Mark and Spencer kindly sent to me about the lovely Suzie (it will lighten the mood, I promise!). When Mark and Spencer first brought Suzie home, they had to cover the lounge floor with old duvet covers for much of the time as she wasn't getting the hang of toilet training. She tended to hold on, but when she felt excited or nervous, she would just go there and then, sometimes toileting in her sleep. Within weeks they had bought a carpet shampooer and a big-load washing machine to keep up with her. Suzie had spent some time in kennels at Dogs Trust, so this contributed to the difficulty with toilet training, plus Suzie also had anxiety, which meant that she wouldn't go to the toilet on walks, but would go as soon as they got back; she was just too worried to wee. This meant late night trips out to the back garden for Mark, Spencer and Suzie in all weathers, freezing in their pj's whilst waiting for a wee to happen. This continued for quite some time until one day, Mark made an astonishing discovery. Suzie had pooed in her sleep and had a little on a hind leg that needed cleaning up. Mark was busy washing her leg, the muscly bit just under her bottom, when Suzie squatted suddenly and weed. Just like that! Mark thought nothing of it, but later wondered if the washing down had prompted her. To test the theory, Mark took her into the garden and washed the same place again and, lo-and-behold, she squatted and weed again! Mark then waited a while and took her outside again, this time using his fingers to mimic the cleaning.... and it worked yet again! Mark quickly gave her a treat and praised her lots, and couldn't wait to tell Spencer of this incredible revelation.

When Spencer arrived home from work, he was excited to test out Mark's theory and, would you believe it? A gentle tickle on the back of the hind legs and she squatted and weed again! They were completely awestruck by this incredible event and continued to treat and praise each time she toileted. Please excuse the pun, but after more than a year of toilet accidents, this was an enormous relief! The nights of freezing cold trips to the garden in their pj's became a thing of the past and Suzie soon settled into a reliable toilet routine, otherwise known as "tickling her bum". Suzie still needs the odd tickle to prompt her, but otherwise she is a big girl now and goes all by herself. Luckily, Suzie's "GO button" will work anywhere, so Mark and Spencer can take her to places without worrying that she will make a puddle on someone's floor or in the car. Their friends and the vet are highly amused that Suzie has a "GO button" and are regularly stunned by her party trick, but it means that she has a healthy routine which has opened up opportunities to visit new places, giving some peace of mind to Mark and Spencer.

Suzie is a very special girl, definitely one of a kind. In case you are wondering, I'm afraid it is highly unlikely that your hound will also have their very own "GO button," so be prepared to make do with the less exciting and rather more traditional method of toilet training.

Suzie

CHAPTER FOUR

TRAILIE TALES: TRIALS AND TRIBULATIONS!

Pet name: Harry
Racing name: Foxparke Honky Tonk
A.K.A. Bing Bong, ("the sound his one brain cell makes when he runs about!") Barry, Harry Botter
Date of birth: 28th January 2015
Adoption date: 10th December 2016, from Dogs Trust.

Harry

When Amy and Kayleigh visited the Dogs Trust, they saw Harry just as they were about to leave. He was standing on his hind legs, jumping about to gain their attention, as if to say, "pick me!". Ten days later he was in the car, travelling up the country and on his way to start his new life with them.

Amy says that adopting Harry is definitely the best thing that they've ever done, although it wasn't all plain sailing. Harry was quite nervous initially, and they were worried they couldn't give him what he needed; they felt almost as though they had failed him. Amy describes Harry as a cheeky hound who is good at spooning. He particularly enjoys wearing the dustbin lid as a necklace and then parading it around the house and garden while they attempt to retrieve it. Recall has been a challenge; Harry had to do "dog school" three times!

On one occasion, Harry was tempted by the appeal of a run on nearby farmland and evaded both Amy and Kayleigh while they were training him together. On another occasion, Amy approached Harry in a doorway to clip on his longline, when the door swung and hit her, knocking her unconscious. The door was open and Harry was unattached to the longline, so he took full advantage of the situation and ended up four miles from home! Amy was very late for work that day.

Like many of the hounds, Harry is a keen jumper. Amy and Kayleigh decided that nine-foot fencing was necessary in order to contain Harry and his exuberance safely, the downside being that they appear highly unsociable to the neighbours!

Pet name: Reggie
Racing name: Tyne View
Date of birth: 9th March 2017
Adoption date: re-homed 26th November 2019 from Worcestershire
Animal Rescue Shelter.

Reggie

A Trailhound was first suggested to Sharon by a kennel assistant at
Worcestershire Animal Rescue Shelter, when she visited to see if

there were any suitable dogs needing a home. Sharon knew little about the breed, but was assured that they make great pets and love their home comforts. A few visits to see Reggie and some ball games later, the family fell in love with this handsome chap with a silly bark! Not long after they brought him home, the same evening, in fact, they realised he was a wild dog! He jumped onto the kitchen worktop and table, stole bread from the sideboard and toileted in the children's bedrooms.

The family hadn't had Reggie for very long, when they were out exploring the village with the hound and came across the local campsite. Towering high above the entrance, they were drawn to the spectacular views of British Camp in the Malvern Hills Area of Outstanding Natural Beauty. Eager for more views, they wandered inside to explore. It was a cool, crisp and sunny winter's day; the sky was a clear blue and filled with the sound of birdsong. They ventured towards a pond with an island and a jetty, noticing that the water was covered in green pond moss, which looked like grass. Reggie was keen to take a closer look, so they followed him as he sniffed around and walked out to the end of the jetty. However, when the family reached the end and stopped, Reggie kept walking and made a huge SPLASH! as he fell into the water. He disappeared out of sight for a moment, then bobbed up to the surface with no sign of panic; he calmly swam back to the side and casually climbed out, cool as a cucumber. The family were quite shell-shocked, yet Reggie simply shook himself off and continued his sniffing. Reggie was unperturbed by the whole experience and quite enjoys his sessions in the pool with Sharon, a canine hydrotherapist.

Reggie's family recently took him snowboarding and videoed themselves having fun together. They later posted the video to Instagram, and it was spotted, leading to a television appearance on Ski Sunday! Reggie can be seen hurtling towards the camera at top speed and then disappearing just as quickly in the opposite direction.

Pet name: Robbie
Racing name: Mister
Date of birth: 19th February 2011
Dam: Quiet Pearl, Sire: Westgate Kyza
Adoption date: re-homed from Canterbury Dogs Trust November 2013.

Robbie

Elaine tells me that Robbie is a very chilled out hound who was already well trained when he came to live with her, with surprisingly good recall! He is Elaine's running partner, and they have taken part in five Race for Life events together, as well as doing a little canicross. Robbie is occasionally a bit less enthusiastic when the weather is warmer, becoming a somewhat reluctant runner. He likes to have a little lie down on the job and it takes copious amounts of tasty morsels to tempt him; this is rather counterproductive, as they had taken up running in the first place in order to keep Elaine and Robbie's weight down!

Robbie is completely food obsessed and loves anything cheesy! At Elaine's son's birthday party, the boys had takeaway pizza for tea and then went out to play in the garden. The remaining pizza was left on the kitchen table, much to Robbie's delight. However, instead of snaffling it and eating it in the kitchen, Robbie took two large pieces in his mouth, one hanging out of each side, and brought them into the garden to parade his stolen wares for all to see! Robbie ate the largest piece, while the other was liberated from him, disappointingly for Robbie.

Robbie has supersonic hearing and can hear a cheese packet being opened a mile away, even when he is apparently snoozing. The one and only time that Elaine managed to take some cheese without Robbie realising, was following a twenty-mile walk, when he was fast asleep!

Robbie very sadly passed away on the 17th July 2021, leaving an immense hole in the hearts of his family. He will be greatly missed.

Pet name: Lucy
Racing name: Dallas
Date of birth: April 2002-December 2017
Adoption date: re-homed August 2003 via Lakeland Trailhound Trust, from Faith Animal Rescue.

Lucy

When Jane met Lucy, it was Lucy that chose her, rather than the other way around. Jane describes Lucy as a failed racer who enjoyed sofa surfing and bed-sharing, when she wasn't running off! Lucy's recall was an absolute nightmare and there were lots of off-lead escapades. Whilst trying to train recall, Jane had to chase Lucy across a large country area in Hertfordshire, trying to keep up with her. Jane could hear drivers beeping their horns and could see headlights flashing in the distance; she later found Lucy trotting along, following the white line of a service road, while exasperated drivers tried to pass her. On another occasion when Lucy disappeared, she was found sitting with a family having lunch in a pub garden! At this point, Jane realised she really must enlist the help of a dog trainer. Having had dogs in the past which stayed close by on walks, Jane realised that hounds were a bit different and just wanted to follow their noses; Jane remembers fondly that she did lose weight, but the training was a success in the end!

When Lucy was being looked after by Jane's daughter, Lucy managed to polish off a large bag of Hotel Chocolat drinking chocolate, which resulted in a large vet bill and stomach pumping on Boxing Day. Jane's daughter was panicking and had to phone Jane to let her know while she was away on holiday.

Lucy was the best travelling dog and spent numerous hours in the car, covering many miles in Europe and across the UK. She took ferries, trains, hotels and campsites in her stride, but heaven forbid if her tea was late! Next came Jess:

Pet name: Jess
Racing name: Shameless
Date of birth: January 2011
Adoption date: re-homed via LTW September 2017, following a successful early racing career.

Jess

When Jess came to live with Jane, she had counter-surfed on the dining room table and eaten the fish food within the first ten minutes of setting foot in the house! Six months on, Jane had lost another half a stone while trying to train recall. Jess enjoys jumping, clearing fences easily, and she likes to "pop next door" to have a wander with the livestock, although she isn't very keen on the geese. Jess's first meeting with a large pig resulted in her jumping a five-bar gate to get away.

Jess has been with Jane for three years now and she is a peaceful, well-adjusted hound, with surprisingly good recall. She loves the small grandchildren and has almost given up chasing deer. Jess is much admired and well-known locally, with Jane spending a lot of time explaining what she is. Jess is very spoilt, with a choice of five beds; she is a hopeless guard dog, but well loved!

Pet name: Jen
Racing name: One Day
Sire: Jenny's choice, Dam: Huntsman's Jenny
Date of birth: 24th March 2017
Adoption: re-homed via LTW

Pet name: Suzi
Racing name: Sue
Sire: Free Spirit, Dam: Jenny's Rascal
Date of birth: 15th February 2019
Adoption: re-homed via LTW

Photograph by Susan Smith: Jen

Jen and Suzi are both very good, well-mannered hounds, although Andy, one of Sally's previous hounds, had a few misdemeanours. Sally once took Andy and Cady to a local meadow next to the river, where Andy managed to get away from Sally. He was later found in the queue for the burger van at the football club next door! A few weeks later, Andy absconded again from the same place, only to be returned to Sally by the very nice gamekeeper. Sally was expecting a thorough telling off but instead, the gamekeeper said that Sally was lucky to be getting him back as Andy was so lovely that he wanted to keep him!

Jen really doesn't enjoy getting cold, so when they attend agility classes in the barn during the winter, Jen has to wear two rugs and a fleecy neck warmer with her ears tucked into it and she curls up on Sally's chair because she refuses to sit on the sand.

Jen and Suzi both love washing the cats, paying particular attention to the insides of their ears, which the cats love!

Suzi and Jen

Pet name: Star
Racing name: Miss Tiote
Adoption date: re-homed September 2012 at 18 months old, from
Worcestershire Animal Rescue Shelter.

Pet name: Meg
Racing name: Twilight Mystery
Adoption date: re-homed February 2013
Dam to Meg and Star: Miss Molly

Meg and Star

Following Meg's decision to sit down halfway round a trail, her
racing owner decided that perhaps racing wasn't for her, so Meg
went to live with Clare. Meg loved to play with other dogs, so Clare
soon decided to re-home a second hound. In February 2013, Meg's
littermate Meg came up for re-homing; to Clare, it felt as though it
was meant to be, so Meg and Star were reunited. They instantly
remembered each other and absolutely adore one another!

At times, the strength of their bond is a disadvantage. Clare used to
let them off the lead in the fields near their home, and they would

often find a scent to follow. On Good Friday 2014, they disappeared together and were nowhere to be found. Clare contacted Doglost to report them missing, and they searched high and low for Meg and Star. On Easter Sunday, after an awful couple of days, Clare received a phone call to say that the hounds had been found in the grounds of a local theological college, still together. Clare took them for a check-up at the vet's, but apart from being tired, both were in perfect health and were none the worse for their expedition. Clare felt thoroughly embarrassed by the whole experience, which was not helped by the fact that Star and Meg gained fame and stardom as the hounds in the Doglost posters; they are still recognised, even today! Regardless, Clare finds them both adorable and tells me it is a privilege to have them.

Pet name: Tam
Date of birth: 10th February 2017

Pet name: Eddie
Date of birth: 30th March 2017

Eddie and Tam, both non-racers and well-bonded, arrived at Dogs Trust together and were re-homed to Faith on 30th April 2018. Faith was only looking for one hound, but she couldn't resist taking them both! Two adolescent hounds that had never lived in a house before, combined with two novice dog owners, certainly made life interesting; they had some lively and sleep-deprived weeks! Within two minutes of entering the house for the first time, Eddie was found standing on the kitchen counter surveying his new realm, while Tam found a rather nice rug to wee on. It took a while to achieve a settled household.

Eddie is the more adventurous of the two and, one morning, he went missing. Faith searched the house and what *had* been a hound-proofed garden, with no luck. Within five minutes of him being gone, Faith had started to panic when he came trotting back, with his normally white snout stained orange and smelling suspiciously of oxtail soup. Eddie the bin raider had not only scaled Faith's six-foot fence to find his way back, but also those of four sets of neighbours!

Tam has a talent for tracking down and luxuriously rolling in dead marine mammals that she finds at the opposite end of the beach, meaning that car rides home in winter are far from pleasant!

Eddie

Tam

Pet name: Bob
Racing name: High Challenge
Adoption date: re-homed from Worcestershire Animal Rescue Shelter at seven years old.

Bob had a long and successful racing career, winning the Produce Cup as a one-year-old. Dave says that Bob had the incredible ability of tracking down the smallest of stinky puddles in the largest of fields to have a good lie down in, and when he was lucky enough to be taken out for a coffee, he liked to "pull up a chair" and join the humans. Bob enjoyed being able to see what was going on, including keeping an eye out for any food that he might miss out on; he particularly favoured a sausage sandwich!

Bob's ears doubled up perfectly as a weather vane; you always knew which way the wind was blowing with Bob around. He was a great family pet who was very adept at posing for selfies, often with his mouth wide open to hog the limelight. He also loved to collapse in a heap in an armchair for a snooze, regardless of who might already be sitting there. Bob sadly passed away at twelve years old.

Photograph by Helen Warrington: Billy and Betsy

Pet name: Billy, A.K.A. Big Lad
Racing name: Cracking Thorpe
Date of birth: 12th March 2012
Adoption date: re-homed from Dogs Trust Leeds in October 2015.
Billy had a successful career and won races but retired at three and
a half years old due to sustaining an injury; he later sired a litter.

Pet name: Betsy
Racing name: Paloma Faith
Date of birth: 12th May 2014
Adoption date: re-homed privately September 2018

Denise and Graeme had Boxers prior to Billy and Betsy, but wanted another dog to keep their remaining Boxer company. Graeme persuaded Denise to go for a change of breed; something smaller and more agile that he wouldn't have to manhandle over stiles! Graeme wanted a dog with stamina that he could go running with and that would enjoy caravanning, but couldn't face going through puppyhood again. Denise wasn't keen on Graeme's preference for a terrier and "suggested," rightly so, that a Trailhound was the correct choice. They went to meet Billy, then visited again with their Boxer; within two weeks, Billy was home. He settled in quickly, although the Boxer was rather astonished by the big hound cuddled up on the settee, a privilege which he had never been allowed!

Billy joined Graeme in his training for an Ironman triathlon and later entered a charity canicross event which had an exciting start to it: Billy set off at full pelt and Graeme had to hang on for dear life. Thankfully, Billy slowed down a little after about half a mile!

Graeme and Denise were fortunate enough to make contact with Billy's breeder and previous owners. They met at a trail in Helton, where Billy recognised everyone immediately and was spoilt rotten. Graeme thought it would be nice to walk Billy down to the slip to remind him of his old racing days, but Graeme suddenly found himself holding a lead attached to a D ring, with no Billy on the end. Billy proudly "aroooooed" up and down the slip to his heart's content, looking resplendent in his red harness… until he disappeared across the fells and out of sight. Consequently, the race was delayed, much to Graeme and Denise's embarrassment, both worrying about what the locals must think of the "townies". However, there was nothing they could do except wait and hope that he followed the trail. The trailers were all very laid back about the whole affair and reassured them that Billy would make it back as he knew the area, having raced there before… although there was the time that he didn't come back and was later found at a farm with a bitch….! Oh dear. Four hours of worry and distress later, their newly acquired pet returned, wandering in from the wrong direction, tired and dirty; a very short-lived racing comeback.

Betsy, Billy's daughter, later joined the family, providing Graeme and Denise with matching "his 'n' hers" running partners!

Pet name: Lexie
Racing name: Razmatazz
Date of birth: 7th April 2007
Adoption date: re-homed 5th December 2009 after a year of racing.

Lexie

Helen met her first Trailhound when her sister and partner adopted Archie. He made an impression because of his large size and special ability to reverse up into tall vegetation to make his "deposits"; another talent includes singing along whenever a particular Gwen Stefani track was played on the radio.

When Helen was able to have her own dog, she contacted Eileen at LTW and took a long drive down to the Dogs Trust in Salisbury to meet a pair of hounds, Lexie and Binki, both small bitches with similar markings. Helen walked them both, but there was a definite spark with Lexie. When Helen returned to collect her two weeks later, Lexie and Binki were both in Elizabethan collars because of having been spayed recently. The handler brought Lexie out from the kennels, put her in the car for Helen, and off they went on their long drive home. After about fifteen minutes, Helen's phone rang, and she answered to a panicked voice on the other end of the line. It was the handler from the kennels who apologetically admitted to Helen that he had put the wrong hound in her car and it was in fact Binki who was happily on her way to a new life with Helen! She turned the car around and the hounds were swapped back, leading to endless ridiculing from Helen's family for not noticing.

Lexie took quite a while to adjust to living in a house. On her first night she followed Helen to the bathroom, poked her head around the door to see what she was doing, and then promptly weed on the landing carpet as if to say, "Oh I see, this is what we do up here". On another occasion, Helen took Lexie to her Dad's house and from the garden she looked up and was puzzled to see Lexie framing the conservatory window, her entire body completely visible. Upon investigation, Lexie had jumped up onto the very high utility worktop and was happily helping herself to the cat's food!

After losing Lexie, Helen then adopted Jelly and later, Nutkin. Jelly and Nutkin enjoy "assisting" in everything that Helen does and are both very nosy. Their recent endeavours include "helping" Helen to paint when decorating her house. They offered their services to the plumber when he had his head jammed in a cupboard under the sink, then proceeded to overpower him to give him a good licking; they also enjoy a spot of gardening and dig holes, in case that might be helpful.

Pet name: Jelly/ Jellybean
Racing name: Border Blossom
Date of birth: 22nd March 2018
Adoption date: re-homed November 2019 via LTW.

Pet name: Nutkin
Racing name: Foxparke Peggy-Sue
Date of birth: born 6th March 2014
Adoption date: re-homed August 2020

Nutkin and Jelly

Pet name: Josey Wales/ Joe
Date of birth: 2007
Adoption: privately re-homed

Nikki and Ian soon discovered that Joe had "selective" hearing. Joe enjoyed a good gallivant after a scent, disappearing off into the distance, taking fences and gates in his stride.

Joe

One day he was gone for six hours before he came trotting back into the yard with his tongue hanging out, looking extremely pleased with himself. When Nikki asked a Trailhound veteran how to stop a hound on a scent, she was told to "get in front of him". He clearly believed that Nikki could run at an Olympic speed!

When Nikki and Ian moved away from Cumbria and into a town, Joe particularly enjoyed serenading their neighbours with a tune or two. In 2016, they bought a pet passport for Joe so that he could accompany them on their summer holidays to France. He was the perfect travelling companion and the only reminder of his presence was the noxious fumes which periodically emanated from him, causing an outcry and emergency opening of windows, whatever the weather.

Joe loved to lie in his bed on the terrace of the French holiday home, but he was a terrible thief. Visitors had to be primed and warned to keep a close eye on their ham and cheese baguettes, but many failed to safeguard their meal from him; luckily, the boulangerie was just around the corner. On the terrace was a gas barbeque, housed in a raised fireplace. After using it one evening, the metal grills were removed for cleaning. However, the following morning there was evidence to suggest that they had been cleaned insufficiently because of the paw prints found on the surface. Thus ensued a battle between hound and humans as constructions of mesh and metal bars were adapted in attempts to keep the hound away from it, but there was always the telltale evidence of paw prints each morning. Joe's late-night lickings were finally halted by the construction of a very expensive, large wooden box cover. Joe had to console himself through further baguette burglaries and running up and down the vineyards for hours in pursuit of hare and deer, on the rare occasion that an off-lead foray was risked.

At home, one of Joe's favourite pastimes was to potter around the local park, saying hello to the other dogs and hoovering up any stray sandwiches or crisps. Joe was particularly interested in the school bags and coats that were left by the football goal posts, and if his hunt for food was unsuccessful, he would express his disapproval by casually lifting his leg and weeing on the bags. Consequently, if Nikki and Ian spotted him heading for the school bags, they would quickly intervene. However, one day there were no bags, only a lady with her two friendly dogs and her three-year-old in a princess dress. Joe said hello to the dogs and they had a play together, while the little girl stood and watched. Joe took advantage of the situation and promptly approached and weed on her! A mortifying incident which resulted in much apologising and pacifying of a distraught small child, as well as future walks for Joe on-lead and somewhere other than the park.

Pet name: Jake
Racing name: Solway Mist
Adoption date: re-homed from F.A.I.T.H. Animal Rescue in 2004, aged 4.

Pet name: Darcy
Racing name: Safari
Date of birth: 9th February 2011
Adoption: re-homed from Dogs Trust Canterbury.

Pet name: Finn
Racing name: Mitredale Torment
Date of birth: 11th March 2011
Adoption: privately re-homed via LTW.

When Kim and Mark collected their first Trailhound from F.A.I.T.H. Animal Rescue, Jake was as good as gold sitting in the back of the car, so they thought they would just pop into a pet shop on the way home in order to buy an extra couple of things for him. On returning to the car, they spotted that Jake had managed to relocate himself to the backseat, sitting so proudly and watching them as they approached. At this point, Kim remembered the shopping on the back seat. Kim opened the door to find the perfectly intact empty wrapper of a family-sized pork pie, the rest of the shopping miraculously untouched, although this probably had more to do with the large, visible pie-shaped bulge in his tummy.

Jake

Darcy

Darcy came along next to help their remaining dog Bramble to overcome her grief at the loss of Jake. Kim describes Darcy as quick at running but not so quick at learning, having taken eighteen months to teach Darcy to sit. Darcy does many funny things, but a memorable occasion was a walk to the local woods one day. There was quite a large pond in the middle of the woods, which was covered in a pretty solid mass of green weed. As they approached, Bramble and Darcy came running straight for the pond and before she knew it, Darcy had shot off the bank and was up to her neck in water. Poor Darcy had quite a shock, not having realised that the mass of weed wasn't a solid surface, although Bramble managed to stop before she reached the pond. Bramble the hero jumped in to rescue her and, amazingly, Darcy placed her front paws onto Bramble's back and was towed to safety!

Darcy has a penchant for trouble, and if there is a dog doing something they shouldn't, Darcy is always the culprit!

Finn

Finn joined the gang as a companion for Darcy, as Bramble was becoming an old girl and could no longer keep up with Darcy. Finn is a steady, gentle hound, but does nothing unless he wants to. He is, however, their only hound that has never "done a runner". When he first moved in, his favourite pastime was standing on the dining table or on the windowsills. He no longer stands on the table, fortunately, but the same can't be said of the windowsills. Finn loves to jump up for a hug and holds on with his paws; he would happily go home with anyone that showed him a little attention, as he is a big old softie who makes everyone smile!

Pet name: Marley
Racing name: Meditation
Date of birth: 4th January 2006 to 24th January 2021
Adoption date: retired at 18 months old and re-homed from Evesham Dogs Trust November 2007.

Pet name: Betty
Racing name: Spring Remedy
Date of birth: 24th March 2017
Adoption date: re-homed 26th June 2018 via LTW.

Marley instantly befriended Jane's four-year-old son and Molly the cat. On the first day he came to live with the family, he jumped up onto the dining room table and stole their jacket potatoes from their plates in one quick movement! They had been told that he liked food… but this was an understatement! Since then, Marley has removed several hot pizzas from inside the oven, regularly singeing his eyebrows.

Marley and Betty

On one occasion, they went walking in the local forest and as usual, Marley trotted off to explore. Suddenly, they heard screams and shouts, so they ran to see what was happening, only to find Marley mugging two OAPs who had a rather tasty picnic! This set a trend, and many visitors were regularly relieved of their biscuits, kebabs, crisps, and cups of tea, which Marley was fanatical about.

As a youngster, Marley was very agile and easily cleared a six-foot wall at Jane's in-laws. He was a vocal boy and every day at about half-past three, he would begin his plan of getting an early tea by standing in front of Jane, barking constantly until she caved in and went downstairs to fill up his bowl. Marley was a one-off dog; he was extremely loving right until the end and will be missed terribly.

Betty

Betty wasn't well-suited to racing, as she had far too many other exciting things to do! She instantly bonded and fell in love with Marley, becoming his little shadow and following him everywhere. Betty is a very sociable girl; she loves people and dogs, although is not so keen on cats. Recall is still a work in progress. Unlike Marley, she is very good around food and takes treats (not the stealing kind of "take") very gently. Squeaky toys and tennis balls, however, receive the full-on Betty brutality, battle and destruction treatment...... no squeaky toy has survived more than twenty minutes in their house! Betty loves to cuddle but takes up two-thirds of the bed, leaving Jane and Stu to squeeze in as best they can. This means that it is a constant race to see who can claim the best bit of the bed first. Betty has a penchant for chewing flip-flops, slippers, and generally any other prized family possessions, usually Jane's.

Pet and racing name: Cody Lad, A.K.A. "The Face That Launched a Thousand Ships" and "Professor Lad" (his field of study is apparently hats and other human headgear).
Date of birth: 21st February 2017
Adoption date: 31st August 2019 via LTW.

Hannah enjoys canicross and she also scooters with Cody Lad. He understands cues for setting off, passing and slowing down, but lefts and rights are a struggle, as Hannah and her partner can never remember which is which, so they settled for an all-purpose "change direction" cue instead. Cody Lad is hugely athletic and retains his race training instinct to jump fences. Hannah and her partner discovered this one day when they were idly standing next to a five-foot fence, and in a blink, Cody Lad had hurdled it from a standing position and was patiently waiting for them to join him on the other side.

They now use this talent to their advantage and can activate his trailie superpowers on cue; this came in handy on one occasion when their progress on a walk was halted by a gate which had frozen shut. They tackled this by asking Cody Lad to vault the wooden fence next to it. A walker simultaneously appeared from the other direction, looking very surprised, especially when Hannah vaulted over as well, still attached to the other end of his bungee line!

Cody Lad

CHAPTER FIVE

HOUND HALL OF FAME

Pet name: Katie
Racing name: Spring View
Adoption date: re-homed in 2002 at two years old, from the Borders Association via Trailhound Trust.

Mags and Katie achieved the Kennel Club Good Citizen Gold award in their first fourteen months together, passing all three levels. Katie was the first of the breed to achieve this. She won lots of rosettes in fun dog shows, including Best In Show. Katie also became a Pets As Therapy dog, making regular visits to local hospital wards and residential homes.

Mags qualified as an educational speaker for the Blue Cross and Katie was her "education dog". She was affectionately known as "Princess Katie" by the officials at the education department of the Blue Cross. Mags and Katie worked on the charity stands at Crufts and Discover Dogs; they even met Matt Baker and the Blue Peter team! Katie was awarded her very own cloth Blue Peter badge to have sewn onto her Blue Cross coat, and she made an appearance on the show. Mags and Katie met over eleven thousand local children and Katie was made a fuss of and admired by most of them! Mags also taught a lesson at a Dublin school, making Katie the first dog to work for the Irish Blue Cross.

In November 2004, Katie won the Kennel Club's "doggyoke" at the Discover Dogs show at Earl's Court. She went on to "sing" on BBC Radio Lincolnshire and Radio Humberside, and was also invited to appear on the Des and Mel show, but sadly could not attend.

Katie

Katie was filmed by "TV Look North" but, unfortunately, the footage wasn't aired because she didn't serenade them sufficiently. Following the doggyoke win, the local papers ran headlines such as "The Hills Are Alive With The Hound Of Music," "Canine Crooner Katie," "Doggy Diva," "Hound Is A Lead Singer," and so on.

Katie and Mags travelled lots on the London underground and the buses. In 2005, Katie came 9th in Drontal's National Coolest Canine competition, and in 2006, she was featured in the magazine "The Dog Collection" in a special "Friends In Need" edition. She shared the page with a feature on Renee Zellweger's dog, Dylan, and Katie's photo later appeared in the Beagle edition.

Katie and Mags worked with PRO Dogs for approximately one year, visiting schools and nursing homes; the charity has since folded. They won the national prize of Silver Medal for "Pet Of The Year" from the charity, with Katie being the last dog to achieve this.

Katie

Finally, Katie qualified as a R.E.A.D, (Reading Education Assistance Dog) a US organisation, as nobody was running such a scheme in the UK; Katie was only the second dog ever to be registered. She completed two terms before becoming terminally ill, and Mags sadly lost her at nine years old. Katie was Mags's first Trailhound, her "most amazing dog ever," and is still hugely missed.

Katie

Pet name: Paddy
Date of birth: 4th January 2013 to 15th February 2020.
Sire: Westgate Kyza, Dam: Bonny Lass
Adoption date: re-homed 26th September 2013 from Worcestershire Animal Rescue Shelter. Paddy didn't race as he refused to jump gates.

Eileen at LTW arranged for Paddy to be transported to WARS because Michele wanted a young male hound. She met Paddy at one of their fêtes and it was love at first sight! Michele remembers him fondly as the most handsome dog she has ever seen, and she feels very privileged to have shared a special bond with such a wonderful creature.

Paddy was a calm boy, and they shared a mutual trust in each other. Michele was able to take him anywhere and do anything with him; he was not phased by fireworks, gunfire or thunder. Michele shared with me a memory of a particular walk on the Worcestershire Beacon, the tallest of the Malvern hills. They were just on their way down, when Michele spotted a large group of school children at the base but, unfortunately, so had Paddy, who shot off from the top at lightning speed. It was lunchtime and Michele was awaiting the screams from the children as Paddy mugged them for sandwiches and raided their lunchboxes. Michele eventually caught up with Paddy and was very relieved to find no evidence of there having been any food around. Michele called Paddy to her and as he walked by Michele's side past all the children, she overheard a teacher saying to the children, "now that is a very well-behaved dog". Michele thought to herself how differently things could have ended, had they been eating!

Paddy

Another incident occurred when Michele and Paddy attended an outdoor tracking afternoon session in a field full of deer and rabbit scents, right next to a main road. The dogs had to be left secured in the cars with the boot open, so that they could be worked one at a time. Paddy often used to sit in the back seat with a harness and seatbelt on, and was quite happy on his own when Michele was out and about, doing the grocery shopping. However, on this occasion, Paddy became bored with waiting, possibly because he could see Michele through the car window. Michele just happened to look up and there was Paddy, galloping towards her! Despite all the tempting scents, Paddy made a beeline for Michele and then stayed with her for the rest of the afternoon. Paddy had carefully chewed right through the seatbelt, jumped over the seats and out of the boot to see Michele.

Michele and Paddy took part in canicross and obedience classes with the Happy Dog Company, and were invited to take part in their Kennel Club Good Citizen Dog Scheme demo team at Crufts on the 7th March, to take their bronze GCDS bronze test. They had to arrive early, even though their test wasn't until 3.15pm, by which point they were both exhausted as it was so busy and noisy. Paddy took it all in his stride and was admired as they walked around and chatted to people about Trailhounds. Michele was very proud of Paddy, who wagged his tail at the people and dogs, completely unphased by the attention.

When she trained at home, Michele found that Paddy would never sit/lie and stay for over forty-five seconds, so she was really dreading this part of the test. However, as the time came for them to take their turn, Paddy was pretty pooped and flaked out on the floor before it even came to the "stay" element, and they passed with flying colours! Michele remembers having to correct the commentator when he announced that Trailhounds come from Canada…..

Paddy

Paddy

Michele and Paddy received much encouragement from the followers of the Facebook group *Trailhound Appreciation Society,* and some ventured out to provide support in person. If anyone would like to read more about their day at Crufts, do look up the group, if you aren't already a member.

Pet name: Bess
Racing name: Chantelle
Date of birth: 22nd March 2010
Adoption date: re-homed August 2011, from Worcestershire Animal Rescue Shelter.

Sarah met her first Trailhounds, Raymond and Nell, at a race in Cirencester, and it was love at first lick! Sarah is a keen runner and when the time came for her to find a second running partner, Sarah contacted Eileen at LTW; Bess came up for re-homing not long after. She stole Sarah's heart early on, delicately picking blackberries from the bushes whilst on a walk before bringing her home. Bess's independence soon shone through as she happily disappeared a few fields away, no fence posing a challenge. Bess is a keen wildlife spotter and an opportunist.

Bess loves canicross; she is calm around other dogs and enjoys a good howl on start lines, which most people think is cute! They have been on the podium many times, with Bess accompanying Sarah to second place in her age category at the 2012 European Canicross Championships, and to Bronze in the mixed age relays. Sarah and Bess have travelled to more events together and made more friends than Sarah ever imagined; she has found a real partner in crime in Bess.

Photograph by Basil Thornton: Bess

Bess and Sarah also do a bit of agility, with Bess usually knowing the course better than Sarah, and is always at least one step ahead. When Sarah makes a mistake, Bess bites her on the bottom through

118

frustration, much to the amusement of spectators, and to the detriment of Sarah's clothes! Early on, a show organiser gave Sarah a special rosette for "showing the most improvement with a hound!".

Sarah and Bess dabbled a bit in scentwork, briefly. Having only previously experienced the odd stolen sandwich and a bag of pumpkin seeds, which resulted in rice crispy-like poo, Sarah was rather dismayed that introducing the "find it" cue paired with cheese resulted in raided cupboards and pockets. This prompted a friend to enquire why Sarah was "giving Bess lessons in thieving," bringing a rather swift stop to their scentwork endeavours.

Bess

Pet name: Lilly
Racing name: Delta Lady
Date of birth: March 2006
Adopted at 18 months old
Lilly was sent to Scotland for re-homing with her half-brother
Laddie (actual name, Sandy) via a contact of Eileen's.

Heather met both hounds and took them for a forest walk together,
which she describes as just like flying a kite. Heather particularly
loved Lilly, who stopped and waited for the kids when the group
spread out, and they brought her home two days later. Initially, they
had all thought that her name was "Lil," but once they were home
and unfolded the paperwork fully, they discovered it was Lilly!

Lilly adored the beach at any time of the day or night. She also
loved to lift her leg on everything she found there while off the
lead, such as picnic blankets, someone's wheelchair, the surf
instructor's bag on the beach…. mortifying! They could rarely
catch her, so deserted beaches are always preferable now.

Every Tuesday evening for two years, Heather and Lilly visited a
residential home for the elderly, when she was about eight years
old. Although big and boisterous, Lilly loved people and was very
relaxed around them, so she was well-suited to the job. They would
stay for about an hour and Lilly would wander around the lounges,
sitting with anyone who wanted her attention. She was a colossal
hit with the residents. Many of her adoring fans kept biscuits from
their morning tea so that they could share them with Lilly.
Occupied armchairs were in real danger of being tipped over if
Lilly spotted crumbs, though!

Lilly

Lilly was very attuned to the residents and would stand with her head in the lap of one particular man every week, while he stroked her for up to twenty minutes at a time. He would tell Heather all about his two dogs that he had left behind when he moved into the home; for him, Lilly's visits were clearly a godsend. Lilly would be taken to the woods after visits so that she could have a run for half an hour as a reward for her patience.

Lilly

Pet name: Woody, affectionately known as Wonky Chops following an operation to remove part of his jawbone in 2016, because of a tumour in the gum.
Racing name: Langdale
Date of birth: March 2008

Woody raced for one season with the BHTA, then retired in 2009 due to not being very good! He came into LTW for re-homing and Sue kept him as a companion for Lotty, whom Sue sadly lost at the grand old age of sixteen in 2016. Woody has been an ambassadog for LTW for several years and accompanies Sue to shows and fundraising events to help promote the breed. Woody makes a great foster uncle to many hounds who stay with Sue prior to being re-homed. He shows them the ropes and loves to go on long walks on the fells with them.

Woody has been into school to help Sue deliver a talk on the importance of being kind to animals, discussing grooming, training, poo bags, and all that is necessary for a happy and healthy pet. The children were very keen to meet Woody, and there was lots of fussing and stroking. Unfortunately, that was the day that Woody's summer moult started, so there were an awful lot of hairy children afterwards.

On one occasion, Sue, Woody and Lotty met up with Ben, Cassie and Jenny for a run at Golden Valley Common, on the Malvern Hills. Woody was so excited to see Ben's Mum getting out of the car that he leapt up at her, got in a tangle with his leg and head looped through her handbag, and promptly raced off with it around the common, dragging it through the wet and mud. It was rather a brown, gooey mess by the time it was returned to his Auntie Laraine.

Woody used to enjoy agility when he was younger and went to his first competition in Scotland, where there were nearly one hundred dogs competing. In Woody's first two classes, he seemed to forget all of their training and raced around the course, ignoring Sue, and randomly jumped whatever he wanted! He also squeezed through a gap in the fence to run over and say hello to a cute little Bichon Frise. While he was on the wrong side of the fence, Woody thought he may as well introduce himself to the judge and leapt up, planting his paws on his chest, almost knocking him over. Woody really loved the tunnel, so he did it twice, just for fun, and then went to greet a couple of stewards who were sitting nearby, clambering all over them. As Woody suddenly realised that his partner in crime in the car was missing out on all of the fun, he shot off to the carpark to retrieve her. Woody was rather puzzled by the new hand signal Sue was using, very unlike her usual agility signals and cues, consisting mainly of placing her hands over her eyes, lots of groaning and saying "oh no, oh no, oh no" rather a lot. How confusing!

After notching up a rather impressive amount of penalty points for rounds one and two, Sue was given permission from the judge to carry a sausage incentive for the third class, which went much better, although the fourth was his crowning moment, coming fifth out of twenty-two dogs; he even won a rosette!

Woody's chief priority in life is to find things to eat, the more disgusting the better. He is also not remiss to the odd sneaky lick of a passing ice cream if it is at a convenient height, either. Woody has been known to ambush unsuspecting people having picnics on the fells, often partnering up with Meg for maximum mayhem.

Woody

Woody

Meg and Woody

Pet name: Whispa, previously known as Bella.
Racing name: Uptown Girl
Date of birth: 15th January 2011
Adoption date: re-homed 9th June 2013, from Dogs Trust.

Whispa

When the Blakes met Bella, she was a quiet girl with chocolate-coloured splodges on her body, so they felt the name "Whispa" was a better fit. When they brought Whispa home she had been recently spayed, so they were advised to keep Whispa nice and calm, with no strenuous activity. Well, Whispa had other ideas, of course. The first time the doorbell rang, she took off up the garden, vaulted the seven-foot gate and found a group of kids at the corner shop, who fed her with sausage rolls! Whispa was quickly located and thankfully, her stitches were all still intact.

Whispa loves the sofa and to ensure that she has the best seat, her favourite trick is to pretend she wants to go out in the garden, or she runs upstairs. Once the sofa has been vacated by the humans, who have stood up to cater to her every whim, Whispa then races back to claim the warm spot! If her cunning plan is foiled, Whispa communicates her feelings of disgust with a long, loud huff.

Whispa has an excellent sense of (tea) time and likes to let the neighbours know when it's six o'clock, by rousing herself from her prime spot on the sofa and then loudly singing the song of the starving Trailhound until she is fed. Her "hawoooooo, hawoooooo" is the cue for the other three dogs to join in with a chorus of howls, barks, grumbles and snorting; a delightful daily rendition which showcases their rather impressive vocal virtuosity. Trying to explain to her what happens when the clocks change is simply a lost cause.

Blake family house rules:
- Never leave your cup of tea unsupervised. Failure to comply results in tea splatters up the wall, across the arm of the sofa, and an empty cup, except for the rather attractive long string of clear, sticky fluid. Then there is the task of making another that hasn't yet been "Whispa'ed".
- Never leave any food out on the kitchen surfaces. Whispa once helped herself to an entire frozen, still-wrapped pizza, even eating the cardboard base and wrapping. She may have received help from the family collie, but the jury is still undecided.
- To prevent unauthorised refrigerator raids when the hound is unattended, the kitchen broom should be wedged between the fridge and the kitchen counter to activate your very own handy hound security system.

Whispa was given the opportunity to turn her paw to flyball, and although it took two years of training to achieve some sort of consistency in her performance, she soon become known on the flyball circuit as the only Trailhound to take part in the sport, but also the most entertaining to watch. At her first competition, all the dogs were lined up ready to go, the excitement building. The teams shouted, "ready?! ready?! ready?!" to wind the dogs up for a fast start, while they waited for the lights to turn to green. The first and second dogs made great times, putting the team in the lead. Whispa was eager to run and shot off up the lane extremely fast, the fastest she had ever been seen to run. She jumped the flyball box, dodged the person box loading, jumped the four-foot fence around the ring as though it was nothing, and sat begging at the burger van at the far end. She almost took a hotdog from a child's hands, prompting an eruption of laughter from the crowds. Burger vans ceased to be allowed so close to the ringside at future competitions, and a polite request to hide your food whenever Whispa was running became standard practice. At another competition, she seemed to revert temporarily to her trailing days, jumping fences and walls until she was nothing more than a tiny speck on the horizon, much to her family's embarrassment. A mix of sweaty, smelly cheese and fish was the only way they could entice her back.

At a Championship qualifier, the family pulled up at their campsite and let the dogs out of the car while they unpacked the tent. Whispa took one look at them and jumped straight into the nearest caravan, made herself comfortable on their sofa and refused to move. Thankfully, the caravan owner found this hilarious and even served Whispa with bacon and a cup of tea! This was the beginning of a flyball race day breakfast tradition of tea and bacon, sometimes with toast, because if Whispa didn't have this, the team would lose.

Whispa

Because of Whispa's wonderful temperament, the family felt that Whispa would excel at being a Pets As Therapy dog. From the first visit, Whispa had her favourites, such as the lady with the handbag who always saved a few digestives from the tea round to give to her. Her friend found it incredibly funny that Whispa's first stop was always to put her head into the handbag.

There was another lady that Whispa liked to visit who was bed-bound and found it difficult to communicate or do things for herself. Although PAT dogs aren't supposed to do this, Whispa entered the lady's room and jumped up on her bed to snuggle in, making herself at home in the bed with her. The lady loved it and grinned from ear to ear, something which the carers had not seen before. After a few visits, she could pass treats through the bed rails to an appreciative Whispa, who was later taught to put her paws up on the rails as a more acceptable behaviour for a PAT dog.

Whispa is now retired from flyball, but still does PAT visits whenever possible. She is getting on in years, so she dedicates her days to lounging on the sofa and being served tea.

Pet name: Mr Ben
Racing name: Mr Ben didn't make the grade for racing as he found alternative trails more interesting, so was not given a racing name.
Date of birth: 14th January 2013
Adoption date: re-homed from Worcestershire Animal Rescue Shelter 6th December 2013.

Mr Ben

Lucy contacted Eileen Robinson after losing her Springer Buddy in May 2013. There were no hounds available locally (Chesterfield) but two hounds, Ben and Moss, had only just been transported to WARS that week and were in quarantine. Lucy travelled down the following day and met Moss, who jumped straight up, and although he was beautiful, he was as tall as Lucy, so she thought he might be too much for her to handle. When Ben came bounding over, he wasn't sure what to do when he reached her so he just stopped, until she bent down to make a fuss of him; she knew right then that this smaller hound was the one for her.

They had a very long journey home as they were held up on the motorway because of overturned lorries caused by storm Xaver. Ben started off in the boot but ended up climbing into the back seat mid-motorway (Lucy hadn't realised at the time that he should have been secured safely and legally).

When he first moved into his forever home with Lucy, Ben was very confused, as was Lucy's friend, whose husband is also called

Ben. When Lucy regaled her with Ben's antics, this prompted her to refer to him as "Mr Ben," as it saved any confusion when she told of him breaking out of his crate, opening bedroom door handles, chewing hair straighteners and jumping onto her bed! Lucy never quite knew what to expect. Once when she came home, Lucy found him standing in front of the TV, howling along to the Russian National Anthem at the Winter Olympics. Perhaps Lucy's semi-detached neighbour didn't find this nearly as funny as Lucy did.

It took a while for Mr Ben to settle into living indoors and his new way of life, but he adapted really well and became a great running companion. He adopted the local running club "Wingerworth Wobblers" and loved setting off at a faster pace than any of the runners were physically capable of until he tired; Lucy had to run at full pelt to keep up with him until a bit of the excitement had worn off! Mr Ben helped Lucy achieve her first Canicross Female Winner title for a couple of local 5k's at Ashbourne and Thoresby Hall.

Lucy took Mr Ben with her to meet Martin for their first date, almost seven years ago. They went for a walk in the Peak District and stopped off at a pub for a drink and a snack. Lucy nipped to the toilet briefly and when she returned, Mr Ben was standing on the picnic table in front of Martin, eating the chips! Martin wasn't sure how to deal with him, but Mr Ben didn't seem to mind and wore a smug look on his face; they have all been together ever since. Mr Ben knows who the strict one is and who is the easier person to manipulate!

Mr Ben soon took it for granted that every time Lucy went for a run, he should accompany her. Lucy attended a local 5k event a few years ago, and Martin and Mr Ben went along to spectate. On the first lap of the three-lap course, Mr Ben looked a little bored and vacant as Lucy ran past; on the second lap, Mr Ben noticed that Lucy was running without him. After continuing for about two hundred metres, Lucy heard a familiar jingle and thought to herself wistfully, "oh, someone is running with their dog. I wish I was." Suddenly, Lucy was overtaken by Mr Ben, who had slipped both his collar and Martin, having decided to join the race! With the help of a couple of runners, they managed to rugby tackle Mr Ben and secured him until Martin came running up with the lead and empty collar, looking slightly embarrassed. Lucy reports that she didn't achieve a very good time for that race…

Mr Ben has helped Lucy train for her first (and last) marathon and some long distance fell runs. He also accompanied her for Run Every Day January 2018, where they raised money for MIND charity. Mr Ben has been an "ambassadog" a few times, visiting prospective Trailhound re-homers and showing them what being owned by a Trailhound is all about, mainly by chasing the resident cat, jumping up on the settee and howling at the humans. Thankfully, they all seem to have found it endearing and entertaining so far!

Mr Ben has taught Lucy that having a Trailhound is lots of fun, love and embarrassment, with happy memories along the way. Lucy says that she found her best friend with Mr Ben (I'm sure she meant to include Martin, too).

Mr Ben

BLOOD DONORS

Cassie, aged 10, retired from blood donations aged 9.
Wallie, aged 7
Finn, aged 4

Barbara kindly explained the process of donating blood and she tells me that the staff at the RVC are brilliant at putting the dogs at ease. Cassie, Wallie and Finn have always been so excited to go in, as they know that there is food at the end! During these Covid-19 times, they have been going in on their own quite happily, whilst Barbara waits outside in the car. Her Trailhounds were all screened before enrolment to ensure that they would be comfortable with the process and are healthy enough to do so. They also identify their blood type, with all three being DEA1 negative (DEA stands for Dog Erythrocyte Antigen). Only about thirty percent of dogs eligible to donate in the UK have DEA1 negative blood type, so demand for this is high because it can be given to any dog in an emergency. They visit the same blood donor room each time to promote a relaxed environment and there are three dedicated nurses, so they see a familiar face each time.

To donate blood, dogs need to:

- Be aged between one and eight years old.
- Weigh more than 15kg.
- Not have received a blood transfusion themselves.
- Be healthy and not on medication.
- Have yearly vaccinations, regular worming and flea treatment.
- Be comfortable with people.
- Not have travelled abroad.

When the dogs arrive to donate, they are weighed and a small amount of blood is taken from their back leg to check their blood oxygen and iron levels. The vet always gives them a physical check-over by listening to their heart, checking their teeth, and having a top-to-toe feel for any abnormalities. A small patch of fur is clipped from the neck to enable cleaning of the area and to see the vein clearly. A note is always made of which side of the neck the blood is taken, so that the other side can be used the next time. A local anaesthetic cream is applied to the area to minimise sensation, and then they give blood in exactly the same way that humans do. They are laid down on the bed and usually lie quietly, as they are being made a fuss of! The needle and line are then put into the neck and the blood is drawn until the required amount of blood is taken (the amount is calculated by the weight of the dog). Wallie sometimes becomes a little warm and fidgety towards the end, while Cassie used to doze off. Finn has a tendency to want to roll over for a belly rub; not ideal with a needle in his neck! On average, blood donation takes five to seven minutes and the whole appointment lasts approximately forty-five minutes. When finished, they remain lying down for a short while and an elastic bandage is applied to the neck. Then comes the most exciting bit, as far as the hounds are concerned: a nurse fetches them a light meal! As you'd expect, this is consumed in seconds, with the plate left sparkly clean!

I'm sure you agree these hounds deserve a special mention amongst the sporting achievements and charitable activities; they are superstars in their own right.

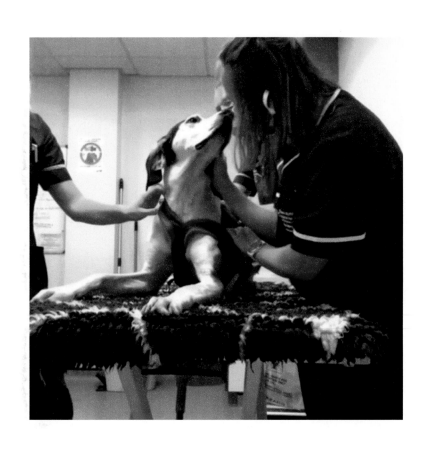

CHAPTER SIX

INTRODUCING TRAINING, NEW EQUIPMENT AND EXERCISE

Before walks are considered, the dog should have formed a bond with his family and feel safe in his new home. In the meantime, some initial training of basic manners can begin. As he learns new behaviours which earn him treats and approval, he will gain confidence and enthusiasm for learning new things. When looking for new equipment, it is important to ensure that it fits properly, doesn't cause any discomfort or restriction of movement, and the dog is happy to wear it. We need to condition anything new before use so that we can build a positive association with it, rather than just expecting the dog to tolerate it; this process can be integrated into fun training sessions. Trailhounds will probably not have worn a harness before, and anything new that isn't introduced properly could be aversive, potentially causing fear and panic. Any existing worries around wearing a collar or harness can also be worked on by replacing them with new ones and working through the conditioning process again.

According to the Control of Dogs Order 1992, "every dog while in a highway or in a place of public resort shall wear a collar with the name and address of the owner inscribed on the collar or on a plate or badge attached to it". However, it is recommended that dogs wear a harness due to scientific evidence that attaching a lead to even a padded or wide fitting collar poses a risk of injury to the delicate structures found in the dog's neck, including the thyroid gland, mandibular gland, trachea, oesophagus, lymph nodes, veins, arteries and nerves. Compression and restriction of the neck area can even cause eye problems because of intraocular pressure. A common misconception is that the dog's neck is tougher than our own, with a thicker layer of skin, but it is, in fact, much thinner and far more sensitive than the human neck. When training recall, it is always wise to use a longline as a safety measure, which should only be attached to a harness and not a collar, to prevent injury if the dog reaches the end of the line, particularly at speed; this is another reason to buy a suitable harness.

Selecting and buying a harness is often not a straightforward task because of clever marketing ploys and sales pitches. There are numerous harnesses available that are described as anti-pull or no-pull, but they are aversive due to how they function; they restrict movement and tighten on the body to stop the dog from pulling. Please bear in mind that no piece of equipment will teach a dog to walk nicely, only training will achieve that. Anything that is described as working like magic or has instant results to help a dog walk nicely should be a huge red flag to you, because it will inhibit and suppress behaviour through being unpleasant to wear. Look for a well-fitting Y shaped harness and use with a connector to the collar for extra security. A double-ended lead with one end attached to a front clip and the other to the back clip of the harness can provide extra safety and peace of mind. Fit should be thoroughly checked for comfort, ensuring that there is no rubbing, no restriction of movement, and that they cannot back out of it. There are many designs available and those with a houdini hound would benefit from a harness with an extra belly strap. Use of a longline is recommended so that they have room to move away and have a good sniff; a shorter lead should be used for roadwork. Flexi-leads are not safe to use near or on roads, for obvious reasons; they can also frighten the dog if they are dropped or dragged, and they often make loud clicking noises. The constant tension will also make loose lead walking impossible. However, if you are walking in a wide-open area with no potential obstacles, they can be handy to allow a bit more freedom if you don't feel comfortable handling a longline.

Come Home Jack in his Non-Stop Ultra harness.

TRAINING TREATS

When choosing the right food to train with, it should always be something that the dog really likes, as opposed to something that we expect them to like or something that someone else has recommended. It is also a good idea to have a selection of treats of varying value so that you can match the treat to the task. Example: My hounds fall into a state of bliss for a well-known squeezy cheese brand, so I use that when counterconditioning to dog walkers, as it is extremely high-value for them (counterconditioning requires the chosen food to be used with a particular trigger and nothing else). When I do simple scentwork exercises in the house, where there are no distractions, I use kibble from their daily food allowance (I use something of higher value when introducing a new task). If I'm going to do the same exercises in the garden, except the neighbours' kids are bouncing on their trampoline, I need to use something much higher value to motivate them, so that would require something like sausage. When we go to scentwork lessons where there are other dogs and people present, I need to increase the value again, so I use cooked beef steak. To see how my hounds rate and value each food, I offer them a variety to see what they do and don't gravitate towards, working out a scale of "like" to "live for" by offering a couple of foods at a time; this enables me to build a picture of their preferences. A top tip is to always hold something in reserve for the occasion when you need something that will trump all other treats. When your dog is performing reliably, has thoroughly learned a new task and can do it easily, you can gradually decrease the value of the food so that the level of reward matches the level of difficulty.

CONDITIONING A HARNESS

You will need:
- High-value treats.
- A quiet, low-distraction environment to work in.
- A harness.

Please do not attempt to put the harness straight on the dog. If the dog avoids the harness, do not chase him; you need to make a good first impression. If your dog is wary of the harness or you can't trust yourself not to move it towards your dog, sit on the floor rather than standing, placing the harness on the floor. Throw a treat away from the harness when your dog shows any interest in it, glances at it or sniffs it. Repeat this until he is approaching with confidence and you are seeing loose, happy, wiggly body language; you can then move to the next step.

Hold the harness in your hand, low down, and without moving it towards the dog. Again, throw treats away from the harness when the dog approaches, and repeat when they return for another sniff. When he is consistently enthusiastic, you can progress to the next step.

Hold the harness away from you and throw treats away from it when your dog approaches. Continue until he touches it, then throw treats away as before. As his confidence increases, you are ready to think about him putting his nose into it.

Hold the harness up as before, hold a treat just inside the opening and give him the treat when his nose is just inside the loop, close to the treat. Then throw a treat away from you to "reset." Repeat the process, making sure that you hold the harness still, so it isn't moving towards the dog. When he is fully comfortable with this, it's time to try it without using a treat as a lure.

When not using a food lure, make sure that you feed him as soon as he voluntarily puts his nose into the loop, even if it is just a tiny bit. Feed in position and watch for any signs of discomfort, which would signify that you're progressing too fast. Throw a treat away from you to reset and repeat. When he can do this consistently, the next step is to wait for him to put his nose in a little further, and then feed again while in position. Throw a treat away to reset between each repetition.

Continue the process in small steps so that he gradually moves a

145

little further into the harness. Once his head is consistently being placed into it, you can start to build a little duration by feeding in position for a few seconds before resetting. Once he is moving far enough to put an ear through, wait for that moment before rewarding, and continue feeding as you remove the harness, to ensure that part goes smoothly.

Finally, reward when both ears and head go through the harness loop. Meanwhile, if your dog tries other things to win the food, just put the harness down, have a break and try again. Continue the process of head in, feed and reset, until he is reliably putting his entire head in each time and is happy to do it. The next stage is to lower the harness onto the neck.

Hold the harness up as before, and when the dog puts his head in, gently lower it onto his neck very briefly and feed as you remove it. Throw a treat away to reset and repeat the process until it is going smoothly.

The next part of the sequence is: head goes in, let go of the harness, touch the strap, and feed as you remove the harness. Watch to ensure that he doesn't avoid your hand as it moves towards the strap, and remember to reset between repetitions, as before. When he is happy with this, you can progress to lifting a strap up into position, as if you are going to clip it, and then feed. If he moves away, stop what you are doing and try again. Ensure he is fully comfortable with each stage before progressing.

The next step is to lift the strap on one side and touch the clips together, let go and then feed. Repeat the process with each clip. Once comfortable with this, it is time to do one clip up, feed and unclip, then repeat on the other side. The last step in the process is to have both clips done up, feed, and then undo.

Gradually increase the time that he wears the harness; don't leave it on for too long and ensure that it is always a positive experience. When adjusting the harness, start with the straps done up loosely so that he has time to get used to the feel and the pressure on his body. In order to free your hands for making alterations to the fit, either use a licki-mat to occupy him, or enlist the help of a family member to feed treats. Eventually, it should fit snugly so that he can't slip out of it but remains comfortable, always in accordance with the manufacturer's instructions. When the harness is on, enjoy some fun activities and feed treats to continue building the positive association.

SKILLS TO TEACH BEFORE VENTURING OUT

When your Trailhound comes to live with you, there is a strong possibility that he will have no training in loose lead walking or recall. You will have gathered by now, from the Trailie Tales chapter, these skills are not amongst their strong points! A harness, longline, some tasty treats and bags of patience are going to be needed. Safety must always come first, so never take risks by letting them go off-lead until you have thoroughly trained for this, please. Behaviour which is practised becomes stronger and will become a default choice, so safety and management must be paramount; running off after a scent is also hugely reinforcing! Make use of secure fields for hire in your area and be aware of any potential distractions while you are training. If you know the area you want to use is frequented by loose dogs, deer or rabbits etc, there will be little chance of them being able to focus on you and any learning. Once their nose is engaged, they simply cannot hear you, no matter how much you shout for them to come back. Start practising anything new at home first and build in distractions gradually, always setting them up to succeed.

Dogs do not generalise well, so we need to "proof" the things that we teach them. This means repeating an exercise to reinforce a new cue, and practising in different places and situations so that they understand it applies all the time, not just in a certain setting. Keep

147

training sessions short and don't be afraid to abandon if they aren't going well, or if you or the dog is becoming frustrated.

There are various reasons why your dog may not respond as you would like, so you need to analyse carefully and problem-solve to help your dog achieve the results you are looking for. It is easy to dismiss a dog as being stubborn or naughty, but this is certainly not the case. If you start to feel this way, you need to ask yourself a few questions:

- Has your dog understood what you are asking of them?
- Have you practised enough?
- Have you varied the settings to proof what you are teaching?
- Have you gradually introduced distractions?
- Are you progressing too quickly?
- Are they feeling overwhelmed?
- Is there something in the environment that is worrying them?
- Are you expecting too much?
- Are your treats high enough value to motivate your dog?

Before we go through some training methods for loose lead walking and recall, there are a couple of things that you will find helpful to work on first.

INTRODUCING A MARKER WORD OR CLICKER

Goals:
- To "power up" the chosen marker so the dog associates the marker with a reward.
- To build your own confidence in using a marker.
- To "dial up the dopamine" whilst establishing calmness to enhance learning.

You will need:

- Lots of tiny, high-value treats that can be easily swallowed without chewing.
- Decide on what the marker will be, whether that is a clicker or a word such as "nice" (the dog will process a click quicker than a word, therefore allowing for more accurate marking.)
- A low-distraction area to train in.

Wait for a calm moment, deliver your chosen marker to the dog and reward immediately. Follow the pattern of mark and treat, wait a beat (this will ensure the marker predicts the food). Repeat this for up to five minutes at a time, with several sessions of this per day for several days, or until the connection is made.

Troubleshooting:
If the dog grabs at the food, put it into a closed hand; wait for calm before offering the food. This will teach him that polite behaviour earns him the reward. Wait for him to pause, then mark and reward. Remember that our actions influence the dog, so stay calm and move slowly.

If you have a sound-sensitive dog and you are using a clicker, be aware that the clicker may startle him; you could wrap it in a towel to muffle it until he has formed a positive association with the sound.

How do you know that the dog has made the connection between the marker and the reward? Test the marker. Wait for a calm moment, then mark and observe the dog's reaction. If he looks for his treat, then the marker is "powered up". **Remember: always reward after a marker to maintain its power, even if the marker is mis-timed or used by mistake.**

NAME REFLEX

Your hound may well have several names already, including a pet name, a racing name, and probably a few rather rude nicknames

149

which you may have introduced following a few soggy carpets, swiped sandwiches and muddy feet on your pillows. On the other hand, you may have renamed him completely. Whatever the circumstances, your hound will need to know his name, be able to respond to it and have a positive association with it.

Start in a low-distraction, secure environment. Let him see you throw a tasty, smelly treat away from you. He will approach and eat it; the moment it is gone, call his name. As he comes running for more of the good stuff, throw another treat away from you in the other direction. Again, he will pounce on it; the moment he finishes eating, call his name. This will be a popular game! Practise lots, until he responds consistently.

BUILDING ON THE NAME REFLEX AND INTRODUCING THE BEGINNINGS OF RECALL

You will need:
- A longline.
- A harness.
- Two handlers.
- Tasty, smelly treats.
- A clicker or marker word.
- A chosen cue word.
- A low-distraction area to train in.

Always start in a completely secure, low-distraction environment; it is crucial that your hound does not have the opportunity to practise running off. Always attach a longline to a harness, not a collar, and let him drag the line. If it is doubtful that he will stay with you, hold on to the end of the longline.

Stand a couple of metres away from your helper. Person A should call the dog using his name and then follow up with your chosen cue word once the dog moves towards them. Mark and reward with tasty treats and a fuss when he comes. Person B then repeats the exercise, with treats and praise when the dog comes. Continue so that the dog is running happily from one person to the other, and he will soon learn to associate the cue word with returning for a treat party and fun. You can gradually increase the distance that the dog runs between you.

HAND TARGETING

I found this particularly helpful for my reluctant-returner when we first started visiting a six-acre secure field. Understandably, he wasn't all that keen on having his playtime interrupted to go home, so I needed to inject some extra fun into recall. I started with a simple hand touch and once he could do that easily, I progressed to holding my hand at different angles for him to target, which he found quite exciting. My next step was to offer him my hand when I was moving, which resulted in more excitement. Bingo! He now stampedes across a field to chase me down and target my hand when I hold it out to him; sometimes he is even considerate enough to close his mouth first! I discovered that offering him my hand whilst walking was also a great way to position him next to me, demonstrating that this a very handy skill when teaching loose lead walking.

TEACHING A HAND TARGET

You will need:
- High-value treats.
- A clicker or marker word.

Roll a tasty treat in your hand so that your fingers smell of food and then discard it. Present your open hand to your dog, who will

151

come over to investigate. When his nose touches your hand, immediately mark and treat. Repeat until your dog can do this consistently, then add a cue word (I use "touch," but you could use "hand" or "target" etc.) Pair the cue word with the action of targeting, and repeat until your dog offers the behaviour when cued. You can build duration when they target your hand by encouraging them to hold their nose in place, delaying the marker fractionally. By this stage he should be really keyed into the clicker/marker equals tasty food, and he will expect to hear it.

TEACHING A CHECK-IN OR FOCUS

This is an extension of the name reflex exercise.

You will need:
- High-value treats.
- A clicker or marker word.
- A low-distraction area to work in.

Step one: Call your dog's name and when he turns to look at you, simultaneously mark and treat. Practise until he consistently responds when you call his name.

Step two: Let your dog explore a little, wait until he happens to look at you, and then mark and treat. To prevent him from simply staring at you for food, deliver the treats to the ground or floor. When he is consistently looking to you, add a "watch me" cue.

When your dog can do both steps easily at home and in the garden, practise in other settings. When increasing the difficulty of one aspect of the training, for example, working in an unfamiliar environment, you will need to reduce the other criteria, so repeat both steps to help lower the difficulty, initially.

FURTHER RECALL TRAINING

Please remember that safety and management must come first. Do not turn your hound loose until you have thoroughly trained for it, ensuring that the environment is always safe and secure. When teaching recall, be careful that the lead doesn't become a predictor of the end of play. Vary when the lead goes on and off, vary the environment, your route, and any games which your dog may learn to associate with the lead going on. Be as exciting as possible so that your hound is more interested in you than any distraction, and use high-value treats and any toys your hound likes.

It is a good idea to practise a collar touch to prevent him from disappearing immediately after receiving his treat, when he realises you are going to put him on the lead.

COLLAR TOUCH/HOLD

This can be incorporated into the earlier exercises or taught separately. When your hound approaches for a treat, gently touch his collar as you feed him. Build up the amount of contact with the collar slowly so that he isn't prompted to run off by you reaching for it; close contact and collar touching needs to be a positive experience. To help to position him conveniently, feed the treats between your knees so that he is easy to reach to clip the lead onto his harness.

RELEASE CUE

Introducing a release cue alongside your recall cue is a great way to let your dog know when he is free to play. Reward him for staying close to you and encourage him away by throwing a treat or a toy, adding your chosen cue "free," "go play," or something else to that effect.

I can't stress enough how important it is to have a solid recall and the more tools you have in your toolbox, the better. Practise, practise, practise, and always use a longline wherever possible so that you can increase your dog's freedom while still having a safety net.

LOOSE LEAD WALKING

This is probably the greatest challenge of all, as most dogs are likely to pull at some point, for various reasons. Pulling can occur due to a myriad of distractions in the environment that they will encounter, or it can be caused by excitement, when they are full of energy and want to approach other dogs, or reach a smell. It can also occur when they are feeling overwhelmed or worried, and they might pull, jump up at you or bite at the lead as they try to escape the situation. Dogs do not automatically know how to walk nicely on-lead, and they do not understand what it means if they are pulled back or constantly stopped, which will only cause further frustration for you and your dog. Motivation and reward, alongside kind coaching methods and careful observation, will help your dog to learn what you would like him to do in a positive, yet effective way. The skills that you have already taught for recall will be invaluable, alongside giving your dog plenty of time to sniff.

Try to think of walks in terms of time, rather than completing a particular route. Choosing somewhere quiet to walk will be really helpful, and set out when you aren't pushed for time. Giving your dog the option to have a wander first while attached to the longline will help to minimise frustration, whilst also fulfilling their need to sniff (every single blade of grass they possibly can!).

Loose lead walking needs to start at home, naked, (the hound, not you, although that's optional, of course!) with the skills outlined above being taught first.

You will need:

- High-value treats.
- A clicker or marker word.
- A low-distraction, secure environment to train in.
- A harness with two points of attachment and a 2m double-ended training lead.

Exercise One: Call your dog's name and walk a couple of steps, then mark and treat when he follows you. Move on a couple more steps, giving a cue such as "this way" or "with me," then mark and treat as he comes with you. The lead should be kept loose, so if he starts to pull, change direction and give your cue. Very gradually, increase the number of steps that you take before changing direction, and practise lots. Use a high rate of reinforcement, (lots of treats!) keeping things calm and relaxed, without shortening the lead or pulling. Turid Rugaas refers to loose lead walking as having a "smiling leash," which is a lovely visual aid and a great reminder!

Exercise Two: Repeat as before, but mark and treat when he looks at you. You have already taught your dog to check in with you, so this should be straightforward. Your dog won't be able to pull when he is looking up at you. If you find he is focusing on you too much, deliver the treats to the ground to redirect his attention. Dogs need to enjoy their walks and engage with the environment, so a balance between checking in and having a sniff is important. Placing treats on the ground is also a good way to avoid your dog jumping up at you for food, and it will help to minimise frustration by encouraging him to sniff and explore.

This will need a lot of regular practise at home, in the garden, on the driveway and so on, as well as patience and consistency. However, it is really worth the effort because walks will be so much more enjoyable for everyone concerned, so stick with it and perseverance will pay off. It is a challenge indeed, and those with multiple hounds have probably all felt as though their hounds are attempting to draw and quarter them when they head in opposite directions to each other for a sniff.

When you have thoroughly practised all of your newly acquired skills and your hound is happy wearing his harness, you are ready to venture out. You might find that he is a little overwhelmed at first, because of the change and adjustments he is making. Sometimes it will be necessary to spend several weeks at home before even entertaining the idea of walks, so that the dog can decompress thoroughly. Lots can be worked on in the safety of the home and garden to prepare for walks, including the skills we have discussed so far. In addition, a "let's go" cue is invaluable as an emergency U-turn, when you need to create space and encourage your dog to move away. This is very easy to teach: simply lure your dog with a tasty treat to encourage him to move with you, whilst adding your cue.

When trying to ascertain the right amount and type of exercise, the adopter needs to ensure that the dog's needs are met, whilst considering energy levels. Some dogs are very stressed by their environment and if exposed to triggers regularly, they can suffer with long-term stress, which will affect both their health and wellbeing. The adopter should question whether the dog is fit and healthy, are the walks fulfilling and does the dog like and enjoy them? What does his body language communicate? Despite the common belief that a dog must have at least one walk every single day, this is not the case; it may be better to stay at home sometimes, where the dog feels safe and where activities can be catered specifically to his needs. He needs the right physical and mental outlets, avoiding things such as ball launchers which can fuel obsession, cause overarousal and excessive wear and tear to the joints from repetitive movement.

WHAT IS AROUSAL?

Arousal is the way in which a dog responds to things in his environment because of the state of the nervous system at any given moment, whether that be cues from his human, other dogs, animals or vehicles, etc. Arousal is necessary for the dog to function and can be of benefit to a certain point, but becomes detrimental if arousal levels are too high. Arousal affects how negative and positive events are processed by the dog and the resulting emotion which he connects with those events. Arousal itself is not an emotion, but it underpins the expression of emotion and modifies the degree of response from the dog. Consequently, he may respond in a number of ways to the same trigger, depending on his level of arousal at that time. Arousal affects the dog both psychologically and physiologically, so it is important to regulate it. Behaviour issues can often be attributed to high arousal levels, as the dog can demonstrate "escape behaviours" such as biting, barking, nipping and hyper-vigilance, and generally disconnecting from their handler. These behaviours appear because the dog needs a break, as he can no longer cope. His brain state changes and he cannot think clearly or learn when in this situation. If the dog remains in this neurological "stress zone," it can have long-term physical and mental consequences; neuroplasticity is affected, with these extreme reactions often becoming habituated.

Physiologically, there will be increased pupil dilation, an increased heart rate and blood pressure, suppressed digestion, and blood will be diverted to aid the fight-or-flight response from the sympathetic nervous system. There is an influx of hormones, including cortisol and adrenaline, as well as neurotransmitters. Arousal is cumulative and levels will rise as the dog processes both positive and negative events. An important point here is that fun and exciting activities increase arousal and contribute to stress levels in the same way that worrying experiences do; this is quite a challenging concept to grasp.

THE STRESS BUCKET ANALOGY

The stress bucket analogy is a great way to represent this. Imagine a bucket with a microscopic hole in the bottom to allow the stress levels to subside. The bucket can take quite some time to empty, typically seventy-two hours, although it can be longer. As the dog encounters different stressors, the bucket level rises. If the dog isn't allowed to recover and decompress, the bucket level will continue to rise until the dog reaches his threshold. The moment the dog can no longer cope is the point at which the dog goes over threshold and the bucket overflows. The dog cannot think clearly at this point, as his sympathetic nervous system has kicked in and he is in fight-or-flight mode.

Arousal can be very useful in some situations, such as when learning new things and when engaging in high-energy sports events. With the right level of arousal, there are benefits on a sensory level, such as enhancement to hearing, taste, smell and vision. This is accompanied by increased motor activity and a greater emotional response. Performance increases as arousal levels rise and it boosts thoughtfulness, learning and memory. However, once the dog goes past the point of optimal performance, performance levels will start to decrease as he enters the neurological stress zone. It is important to know that activities which the dog finds fun and exciting also increase arousal, in the same way that worrying, negative experiences do, and will contribute to filling the dog's stress bucket; therefore, it is essential to find a balance. With the aid of decompression, "cortisol breaks" and calming activities at home such as licking, chewing, scent games and quiet "sniffy" walks, arousal levels can be reduced and the dog can learn to relax.

TRIGGER STACKING

It is important to consider the cumulative effect of arousal. If some dogs aren't given the chance to recover from short-term stressors and empty their stress bucket, this can soon cause them to surpass their coping threshold. Dogs cannot rationalise; they have a large emotional capacity but cannot think clearly when feeling nervous or afraid, so it is harder for them to process the onslaught of fear and emotions which distress them. Trigger stacking can occur if they encounter several stressful situations and do not have the time to recover between them. As stress levels can take seventy-two hours to dissipate, trigger stacking is quite an obstacle for some dogs and their humans.

Trigger stacking can give the impression that a dog has reacted to something out of the blue. An example of this is the dog on a walk that passes a bicycle, an off-lead dog, plays a bit of fetch quite happily, but then reacts to something fairly innocuous on the way home. Arousal levels will have built with each experience, and although the dog may seem to have been coping, that small child dragging a noisy toy along behind them may just be too much for the dog; it is the proverbial straw which broke the camel's back.

When first venturing out, times and locations need to be carefully selected and capacity for walks raised slowly. A good starting point is a large, open and quiet space, so that the dog's preferences can safely be assessed, including whether he should remain on the lead or if he can have some freedom. If there is another dog in the household that is reliable, he may provide a lead for the less confident newcomer. It is vital to advocate for the dog and prevent strangers and off-lead dogs from approaching, remembering that an absence of behaviours is not a sign that the dog wants to interact. During a walk, food can be used to test how the dog is feeling: if he is reluctant to take high-value treats, then it is a good indication that he is not relaxed and is feeling stressed. Equally, if he grabs at it or is less gentle than usual, this can signify increased arousal. Cueing a well-known behaviour, such as a sit, is also a good indicator. If he cannot respond easily, then arousal levels are increasing and he will need the pressure to be reduced by adding distance. In these scenarios, recuperation time will be needed to allow his cortisol and adrenaline levels to reduce. Once any triggers have been identified, it is important to have a behaviour modification plan in place to counter-condition and desensitise, along with any necessary medication to provide support.

Having discussed some necessary coaching skills for adopters and their dogs, it is also beneficial to take a training class, such as life skills or scentwork. This is a great way for the dog and their adopter to learn how to understand and communicate with each other, further developing their relationship through taking part in an activity away from the safety of home. The adopter should prepare and plan activities carefully, be patient and understanding, and always seek professional help from a good, qualified professional when needed.

Being aware of any changes which might occur, being consistent in expectations, having environmental management in place and using positive reinforcement will go a long way towards ensuring that the adoption is a success, and will help to safeguard against any negative fallout from any behavioural challenges which may arise.

SELECTING A GOOD, QUALIFIED PROFESSIONAL

Sadly, this is not the straightforward task it ought to be. Finding someone who is well qualified and follows kind and ethical, up-to-date, science-based training methods is an absolute minefield because the industry of dog training is currently unregulated. Scarily, anyone can set themselves up in business as a dog trainer or behaviourist, without needing any accreditations, certifications or experience. One of the biggest myths in the industry, the dominance theory, continues to be perpetuated, despite it being thoroughly debunked. Unfortunately, the meaning of "dominance" in dog training has been blurred and misunderstood. Dominance theory is commonly thought to be based on the belief that a dog behaves in the same way that a wolf would; this belief stems from early, flawed studies carried out on captive grey wolves, to demonstrate how they live and behave within their family unit. One of the first, most influential studies occurred in 1947 under Robert Schenkel of the Zoological Institute of the University of Basel in Switzerland. Although Schenkel's study was very detailed, it was flawed; the wolves studied were not in fact a family unit, but adult, individual wolves that were contained in a small enclosure outside of their natural environment. As the wolves were unrelated, the dynamics and interactions between them differed greatly from those of a family unit living in harmony; the close proximity of other unknown wolves would have been a source of great tension. Schenkel interpreted this tension as competition for rank within the "pack" and unfortunately, this soon transferred into dominance theory for those dealing with and handling dogs.

The results of this study are still drawn on today in order to justify certain dog training methods, and much poor advice is given. This includes, but is not limited to: always eat before your dog, do not let them go through doorways before you, do not allow them on your bed or furniture, all dogs want to be the "pack leader" and are in constant battle with you to attain this role. These outdated beliefs are very damaging to the relationship you share with your dog and can lead to fear, anxiety, and even aggression. However, since Robert Schenkel's study, further research was carried out and in the 1980s, another influential study emerged from American biologist David Mech, highlighting the flaws in the earlier pack and dominance theory. This study was substantial; it was carried out over the course of thirteen summers and reflected the true nature of the wild wolf pack being a family unit which lived peacefully, more akin to a human family.

Although dogs share some similarities with wolves, there are many differences. For example, modern domesticated dogs are more scavengers, rather than hunters. Feral dogs have been observed and even they do not form a traditional pack, rather a "social group," as they enjoy each other's company and interaction. Dogs do what works for them, whether that is to gain their human's attention, to earn a treat, or to feel safer. This is the driving force in their behaviour, rather than a desire to be the "pack leader".

Having delved a little deeper into this subject, it appears that dominance theory predates Robert Schenkel's 1947 study, with many of these ideas actually originating from old gundog training methods from as early as the 1800s. In those days, dogs were not recognised as sentient beings; "breaking" them and submission was desired, and punishment was an acceptable way to achieve this. However, thanks to modern science-based training, we now know better; we know that there is no reason to eat before your dog, as it makes no difference to them. Going through doorways before your dog is only encouraged from a safety point of view and for the sake of manners, but has no bearing on how a dog views himself or his "status". It doesn't matter what position he assumes on a walk, although it is useful to see what he is doing and to engage fully with him, so it is helpful for him to be beside or in front, rather than behind. Ignoring your dog when returning home can cause him to feel stressed; it is much kinder to teach an acceptable behaviour such as a sit, or hand them a toy and then make a fuss. Play can be initiated by either you or your dog. It is important to let him win so that he doesn't become bored, or no longer wishes to interact. Playing tug and allowing him to win frequently can help to build confidence and resilience. It is also a great way to teach him to return a toy to you or take it from you, which can also help build pauses into play to regulate arousal levels.

Behaviour issues have frequently been attributed to "dominance," but when investigated, they often stem from fearfulness. An example of this is the reactive, barking and lunging dog who at first glance appears to be aggressive towards others, but he is simply behaving in this way as a distance-increasing tactic to put space between him and the thing that he is frightened of. It could not be further from the label of "dominance," and would be very damaging to the reactive dog for him to be regarded in this way, in terms of dealing with their fear effectively and kindly. I will take a closer look at reactivity in chapter eight, as it is a topic very close to my heart. The bottom line is that dogs need to be treated as an individual; some will have large personalities, some will not. Occasional problems may arise with dogs of the same sex and the same age, often when coming into sexual maturity. There may be in-fighting between them, as seen in Littermate Syndrome, but it is often a clash of personality or hormones dictating behaviour. Conflict occurs at times, but it most likely stems from pushing the boundaries and learning how to live together, rather than an outdated dominance theory.

Having identified some of the pitfalls caused by the lack of regulation in the industry, we need to outline how to go about selecting someone that you can trust to help you and your dog. The most important point is to find someone who employs reward-based training methods, using food as well as toys and play. Even if a trainer is certified and accredited to a particular organisation, they should still be checked out, ensuring that the professional you hire is actually registered and adheres to the ethos of the organisation. A force free approach is essential; avoid anyone who follows LIMA as it does not rule out the use of punishment and aversives (Least Invasive, Minimally Aversive). Professionals should be expected to keep their skills and knowledge up to date, so check for evidence of continuing professional development.

Some pointers to help you when choosing a qualified professional:

- Always question what methods will be used to train your dog.
- Be aware that "balanced" refers to using all four quadrants of dog training, meaning that they use positive reinforcement as well as punishment or corrections.
- Avoid anyone who is derogatory towards the use of food in training.
- Avoid like the plague if there is any mention of dominant dogs, alpha, pack leader, rank or hierarchy amongst dogs.
- Ask what will happen when your dog does something right.
- Ask what will happen when your dog does something wrong.
- Beware of any references to "correcting" behaviours.
- Beware of anyone claiming to provide results within a certain timeframe.
- Read the trainer's customer reviews for clues to how they train.
- Check their social media profiles for clues and examine photos for any aversives in use.

It is necessary to be a bit of a detective because it is so important that you find the right person to help you. There is poor advice everywhere, both in the professional and public domain. Many people ask for veterinary and behavioural advice on social media platforms, rather than seeking proper help. It is very rare that excellent advice can be distinguished from the many voices often providing, quite frankly, terrible and harmful misguidance. The vet should always be the first point of contact if you have any health concerns for your dog, or if there are any unexplained changes in behaviour; we owe it to our dogs to find them the best help possible, which is both kind and ethical.

CHAPTER SEVEN

THE SCIENCE OF STRESS AND SPOTTING THE SIGNS

This is a subject which all dog guardians should familiarise themselves with because there will always be events which crop up that your dogs might find stressful. It is important to know how to minimise stress as much as possible, by managing the dog and their environment in order to keep them feeling safe. Most Trailhounds are very laid-back and in no time at all, they will be giving your dinner plates the old pre-rinse when you leave the dishwasher open mid-load and your back is turned. However, I feel this topic should be discussed so that everyone has an awareness, at least. Being able to identify the earliest signs of discomfort is an invaluable skill to have in preventing any escalation to deeper stress, and avoiding the behavioural challenges which may then ensue. In order to cover the subject thoroughly, I will talk in more general terms, encompassing dogs which may not have been lucky enough to have had a good start in life.

Stress is not necessarily always a negative experience; for example, it can be of use to a dog when learning something new. The dog may experience eustress, a surge of positive stress hormones which heighten performance and boost their learning capacity. When combined with the feeling of success, some tasty treats and some playtime, this becomes a very positive outcome following short-term stress for the dog. When everything is in balance, eustress can help to build neurons and develop cognitive plasticity, rendering the dog more open to learning and better able to cope with future stressors.

Having said that short-term stress can be a very positive experience, smaller amounts of stress can also lead to a cumulative level which is detrimental to a dog; this usually occurs when the

165

five freedoms are not met. Confidence and resilience levels vary, but if a dog is hungry or thirsty, suffering from malnutrition, is too hot or cold, is in pain, is injured or ill, is isolated or overwhelmed with noise or activity, is subjected to sudden changes to routine, is prevented from expressing natural behaviours or feels anxious or unsafe, he will be susceptible to feelings of stress.

Poor handling and training techniques with a lack of positive reinforcement can be stressful for dogs, as well as being over or under-exercised, not being able to toilet when they need to, and not having somewhere quiet they can go to rest and sleep. There are many situations, objects and environments that a dog might encounter which may cause them varying degrees of stress in day-to-day life, both in the short-term and on a long-term basis. Triggers may include vehicles, fireworks, bird-scarers, or any other sudden, loud noises; babies crying, household appliances, children, strangers, unknown dogs, travelling in the car, or perhaps a visit to the vets. Having no choice whether to interact with any of these objects, situations and environments can be very worrying for the dog.

Stress can occur in dogs even before they are born because fear can be inherited, or it can develop in those as young as five weeks old, following any early negative experiences. This thoroughly quashes the myth that a puppy is a blank canvas. If stress goes unnoticed and untreated, it can persist through to adulthood as they will not grow out of being fearful, and it can often worsen as they mature. Once they reach their normal fear impact period, it is possible that they may never pass through it. Towards the end of the dog's lifespan, the physical decline of his senses, such as hearing or eyesight fading, can trigger feelings of anxiety, and a loss of cognitive function can also lead to increasing levels of stress.

In order to discover what the internal effects of stress are upon a dog, we need to have an understanding of the nervous system and the endocrine system, which are both responsible for the survival response. The nervous system is quite complex, comprising several branches and millions of nerve cells called neurons. Most of these can be found in the brain and spinal cord which form the central nervous system. This allows the dog to interpret and communicate, gaining information from all of their senses, whilst also controlling many internal functions. The other main division, besides the central nervous system, is the peripheral nervous system, and is the more complex of the two. The peripheral nervous system divides into the somatic nervous system, which deals with actions under conscious control of the dog, such as movement, and the autonomic nervous system, which is responsible for the involuntary actions, such as keeping the heart beating, breathing, and digestion. It communicates sensations such as a full bladder or upset stomach to the brain, but also reacts to environmental stimuli and perceived threats, increasing heart rate and tensing muscles, preparing for fight-or-flight. The autonomic nervous system then branches out further into the sympathetic nervous system, the parasympathetic nervous system and the enteric or gastrointestinal nervous system. It is the sympathetic nervous system which handles both mental and physical activity, controlling thermoregulation, heart rate, breathing, digestion, and the fight-or-flight (fear) responses. It triggers the liver to provide glucose to the bloodstream for an energy boost and redistributes blood flow, along with increasing lung capacity by dilating the bronchioles to enable the dog to run away. It also triggers adrenaline production, it increases arterial pressure during moments of stress, and pupil dilation occurs, which is often the first sign of a change to the dog's internal state. Fear aggression is a symptom of the sympathetic nervous system's actions, and once the dog is over threshold, thinking is affected and learning cannot occur. When the dog no longer perceives a threat, the parasympathetic nervous system comes into play to rebalance and bring about the "rest and digest" state. It cues relaxation, stimulates digestion, slows the heart rate down and restores calmness.

It has been discovered more recently that there are millions of neurons in the intestines which form the enteric nervous system, meaning that there is a direct link between the dog's emotions and his gut. What he eats will directly affect his behaviour and impact on his emotions, and every emotion and response will affect the body. The hypothalamus, part of the limbic system and emotional centre of the dog, controls the release of pituitary hormones and regulates behavioural responses alongside basic life functions, and is tied in to the autonomic nervous system. The direct link between the limbic system and autonomic nervous system means that emotions have physical consequences and will affect behaviour. The amygdala, also part of the limbic system, is responsible for survival and defence. Danger or perceived threat messages are sent directly to the amygdala and bypass the thinking area of the brain. Fear increases, as does aggression, and the dog reacts increasingly because his body is flooded by hormones.

Part of the survival mechanism of the fight-or-flight response is the reflex arc, where the body reacts to sudden pain via the spinal cord, without waiting for input from the brain. The sensation causes two signals to be sent simultaneously, one to the affected area so that the muscles can activate and move away from the source of the pain, and the second to the brain, in order to register the risk or thing which caused it. Pain also causes an increase in the stress hormones, and adrenaline is known to have pain-relieving properties, which can mask pain. An example of this occurrence is when you might take your dog to the vet with a suspected injury, but he shows no obvious signs of pain when examined, leaving you feeling rather sheepish and confused, while your dog still isn't quite right.

The endocrine system works alongside the nervous system and is responsible for hormone production through glands and organs found throughout the body. Hormones are chemicals designed to regulate, coordinate and control basic bodily functions. The endocrine system includes the hypothalamus, the pituitary and thyroid gland, parathyroid glands, adrenal glands, parts of the gastrointestinal tract, pancreas, kidneys, liver, ovaries and testes. Input from the nervous system can trigger the endocrine system to produce hormones including cortisol, adrenaline, testosterone and vasopressin. Hormone levels are controlled by feedback loops in the endocrine system, and the body is able to trigger the producing gland to shut off when a hormone is detected at a certain level.

However, when a physical abnormality is present, glands may over or under-produce the necessary hormones and the feedback loops may not always be effective, leading to chemical imbalances, which have clear and important physical signs.

When a dog encounters something stressful, there is an internal reaction which leads to a number of changes within the body, and an external display is present. When a dog begins to feel distressed, the sympathetic division of the nervous system comes into play and the fight-or-flight mechanism is triggered, which in turn affects the immune system, the digestive system, and the dog's hormones. The nervous system and endocrine system take action through electrical impulses and hormones, which are released into the bloodstream to keep the dog alive, beginning with an influx of adrenaline and cortisol to enable the dog to either take flight or fight. Glucocorticoids are released from the adrenal cortex, and the adrenaline and cortisol create a negative feedback loop, which then activates the immune system. Blood pressure and pulse increase, whilst digestion becomes no longer important. There is a flood of glucose from the liver to provide extra energy, and the immune system shuts down so that energy is prioritised for the survival functions.

The dog's response, whether that is flight, fight, fool around, faint or freeze, will depend on the environment, and how the dog has learned to cope when faced with a perceived threat. The first choice would usually be to take flight if he can, with fight normally being a last resort. The initial release of adrenaline may clear from the dog's body within fifteen minutes, but the glucocorticoids released in a secondary phase can take forty-eight hours to six days to subside, and it can take four to six weeks of avoiding triggers to allow the dog to return to a baseline state.

There are many physical signs of stress that dogs may display when under pressure and feeling stressed, some temporary and others longer-lasting. An excess of testosterone and vasopressin are known to have a direct link to aggression, whereas dogs with higher levels of oxytocin tend to be friendlier and less aggressive. Dogs can become noise-phobic, suffer from Separation Anxiety and develop fearful and reactive behaviours; these issues all have a prolonged and exaggerated stress reaction, with serious mental and physical consequences.

The stress response is necessary for survival and normal stress is only short-term and appropriate in relation to the trigger, but if a dog is regularly exposed to multiple triggers, he will suffer physically, psychologically and emotionally and it will lead to lower immunity, poor digestion, poor recuperation from injury and he will be more prone to illness and infection. Longer term stress causes digestion to become compromised, because fewer nutrients are delivered to the cells, and less nutrition means a lower functioning capacity. Stressed dogs feel anxious and are not concerned with eating. When they do eat, they are likely to eat quickly, which means that food won't be properly processed, as blood flow is diverted and digestion decreases. They may also not eliminate properly, which can lead to a build-up of toxins. The endocrine system suffers, which causes a hormonal imbalance, leading to poor behaviour. High levels of cortisol remaining in the body can also lead to shedding of the coat, and skin issues such as dandruff may occur.

With a single exposure to a trigger being experienced by the dog, the effects of the stress reaction can remain for up to seventy-two hours, so repeated exposure can understandably lead to long-term damage if the dog is unable to return to a state of relaxation. If a dog suffers from chronic stress, this can also lead to kidney problems and heart issues. Glucocorticoids sap the immune system and if any medication is administered, this becomes a further toxin and can compromise other bodily systems. Therefore, it is vital to minimise exposure to triggers as much as possible and keep the dog feeling safe so that he can recover both physically and mentally in order to avoid succumbing to chronic stress.

APPLYING THIS KNOWLEDGE TO
YOUR OWN NERVOUS DOG

Interactions with nervous dogs should only occur when the dog actively seeks them. It can be really tough to restrain ourselves, but it is important to wait for them to approach us when they are ready, without attempts to lure them. Luring with food can cause approach-avoidance conflict, by enticing them beyond their comfort zone in order to get the food, causing further worry. Keeping high-value treats to hand, perhaps stashed in strategic places around the house, will enable the adopter to easily reward any behaviours that they wish to reinforce.

There is no set time frame for the development of the relationship with the dog; a trusting bond will still develop without physical contact, and his confidence will increase through observing him from a safe distance. Touch and attention can induce anxiety, so the adopter needs to observe him without placing pressure on him, and should learn to read his body language to enable recognition of the earliest and more subtle signs of discomfort. Any new behaviours arising will indicate a change in the dog's emotional state, but equally, an absence of behaviours can signify emotional shutdown, so the adopter should be as fluent as possible in reading body language. Some signs which may appear include self-soothing behaviours, which are indicative of stress. Any initial over-attentive behaviours towards the adopter which you suspect might be caused by stress, an example being excessive licking, should be discouraged by distracting through play (if appropriate for the dog), or offering a chew and some rest time in his safe space.

It is important to spend time together during the first few days, and he should not be left on his own, initially. He will need to learn how to cope by himself, starting with brief absences and gradually extending them incrementally to build confidence and avoid any anxiety, ensuring that he remains below threshold throughout (no signs of stress). Any following around of a particular person could create an expectation of company always being available, which is unfair, and will not prepare him for or teach him how to cope with everyday life. Too much attention focused towards a particular household member, along with anxious behaviours, could contribute towards separation related problems and possibly resource guarding of his trusted person from other householders.

Observation is key in learning how a dog might be feeling. Body language needs to be viewed in context, from nose to tail. The adopter will need to learn what the dog's neutral, relaxed state looks like when there are no stressors present, bearing in mind that a nervous dog may well show signs of tension in his neutral state. Triggers need to be identified; these will be anything that changes his behaviour due to underlying emotions of fear and stress. When looking for triggers, we need to consider what the dog can see, hear and smell. Scent is a very strong trigger and will be difficult for the adopter to identify; they might see a change in behaviour, but there will be an absence of obvious signs. The adopter should consider what is in the immediate environment and what can be done to reduce the effect of the trigger. Action should be taken to minimise exposure and prevent the fight-or-flight response from being activated, if at all possible. If the dog is faced with multiple triggers, he is likely to remain in a constant heightened state for some time if he receives no respite, so the effects of trigger stacking need to be seriously considered.

FEARFUL BODY LANGUAGE

Fear can manifest in different ways, depending on the dog. How they cope is an individual process; some may bark or climb to seek height, whilst others may freeze or try to escape. Some early warning signals that our dog is beginning to feel stressed include:

- A wide and slow lick of the lips or nose.
- Sneezing or snuffling noises when feeling conflicted.
- Yawning.

- A pinched look to the lips, with tension around the mouth and eyes.
- A closed mouth.
- Squinting or softening of the eyes.
- Whale eye (tension in the face causes the whites of the outer eyes to show).
- Furrowed brow.
- Turn away.
- Freezing.
- Play bow.
- Sitting or lying down.
- Sniffing or scratching.
- Piloerection (raised hackles).
- Panting.
- Shaking off.
- Trembling.

If nothing is done to relieve the pressure on the dog, then he may escalate to more overt signs of stress and discomfort, which include:

- Lowered head or head dip.
- Lowered tail.
- Body or tail may tuck under.
- Tense and rigid muscles.
- Paw lift (this is a fear or appeasement gesture).
- Ears may position out to the side or backwards, giving a pinned back "seal ears" look. The further back the ears are set, the more frightened they are.
- Looking away, turning the head or body away or ignoring.
- Narrowed eyes or blinking.
- Dilated pupils.
- More intense sniffing: a conflicted behaviour, avoiding the trigger and showing confusion or worry.
- Vocalisations. (Remember that nervous dogs may be silent to start with, whereas others may be naturally more vocal).

- Restlessness, inability to relax.
- Sleeping a lot, often due to exhaustion.
- Jumpiness or agitation.
- Hypervigilance.
- Irritability.
- Destructiveness.
- Excessive self-grooming.
- Loss of appetite.
- Hyperactivity.
- Vomiting or diarrhoea.

PROVIDING RESPITE FOR THE FEARFUL DOG

When a dog is feeling stressed or fearful, there will be both obvious and subtle signs of emotion, and he will need to be removed from those situations that he isn't comfortable with. Dogs in flight mode may back away, cower, or try to hide. They will usually hold their bodies low with their head down, ears flat to the head and their tail often between their legs. It is worth noting that this is not necessarily a sign that a dog has been abused. In shut down dogs, they may show very subtle signs: they might shake or shiver, appear small, try to hide, yawn, pant, lip lick, tongue flick or nose lick. Whale eye, sweaty paw prints and submissive urination may also present.

It may become apparent that certain objects or words might already hold negative associations for a dog. Minimising any exposure to potential triggers will help safeguard against new negative associations forming. The adopter should monitor for any fearful reactions and then take action by removing any triggers. They should make a note of the trigger, and there may well be others that need to be recorded; the adopter should then seek professional help, if deemed necessary.

To provide some respite, the dog will need a bunker, in addition to other places around the house where he can go to feel safe. These should be set up in areas where he can have quiet but not completely isolate himself away from the rest of the household, therefore allowing him to watch from a safe distance. If there is another dog in the household that is confident and reliable, he might well provide some support for the new dog, giving him the opportunity to watch interactions and learn by association about his new life and new people. Observing from a safe haven will probably pique the interest and curiosity of the newly adopted dog, allowing him to see the body language displayed by the resident dog, understand what happens during interactions with the adopter, and hopefully he will learn that there is no cause for concern.

Through careful observation we can recognise the subtle, early signs of stress in our dogs. Examples include their use of calming signals and displacement behaviours such as the lip or nose lick, yawning, or displaying a submissive grin, turning their head or body away, looking into the distance, blinking or softening the eyes, moving slowly, possibly in a curve; freezing, sitting or lying down, restlessness, bowing or lifting a paw, sniffing the ground, scratching, or the dog might shake off to calm himself. The whole context needs to be considered, looking for stress-relieving signs and behaviours to appease the perceived threat. If these behaviours do not work for the dog, he may escalate his efforts.

More overt stress signs might include the dog looking for guidance and protection from his human; he may try to climb up them, mouth clothing or the lead, showing what might be perceived as attention-seeking behaviours. He might lunge or pace, pant or tremble, bite or lick himself or bite at and chew furniture, shoes, or anything else nearby. The dog may resort to barking, growling, howling or whining, tail chasing or fixating on reflections or objects. More extreme signs may include diarrhoea or urinating, vomiting or drooling, cowering and tucking the tail under, rolling on his back or crouching over his stomach in a hunched position. The dog might go into emotional shutdown due to overwhelm, or at the other end of the spectrum, he may behave aggressively.

175

Through learning and understanding the signs and symptoms of fear, stress and anxiety in our dogs, we can make life more comfortable for them and ease their distress. We can adapt their environment and routine to suit their needs and ensure that we use only kind, force-free handling in all aspects of their care, including meeting the five freedoms. It is vital to provide comfort when our dogs are scared and understand that any fearful behaviour shown is an emotional response and should not be dismissed as poor behaviour, nor punished. We need to be aware of how we interact with our dogs, being careful not to put them into compromising situations they aren't comfortable with or that they can't cope with. This includes being sensitive to their needs within the home by not causing unnecessary noise which might startle them, remaining calm and trying to stabilise our mood around our dogs, and striving to always be patient with them. It might be a case of soothing them by leaving the radio on, playing something gentle at a low volume to help them feel calm; or if they react to things they can see through the windows, the use of frosted film, or simply rearranging the furniture a little to block access, could make a tremendous difference to them being able to settle at home.

Many dogs dislike direct eye contact from either people or other dogs, so we can help by not expecting our dogs to interact with others that they do not know, or at least approach them on an arc to help them feel safer. Limiting any on-lead greetings to three seconds can prevent issues from arising. Being hugged, kissed, or having their personal space invaded can also be very unpleasant for dogs, so it is necessary to read body language, wait for their permission to touch them, and respect their likes and dislikes.

It is important to monitor arousal levels and understand when your dog is over-aroused through excitement, over-stimulation, hyperactivity, or whether it is fear-based. Learn to recognise and be aware of what your dog's triggers are, and give your dog plenty of space when encountering them. For many situations, such as dog or human reactivity, counterconditioning coupled with careful desensitisation is an effective way of helping your dog, although it takes time and patience (I discuss this in detail later on). Once you have conditioned a positive emotional response to a trigger, it is possible to slowly and carefully desensitise to it, creating new neural pathways while leaving behind less desirable behaviours. Always remain at a safe distance from a trigger; working below the dog's coping threshold is key. Being aware of your own body language, stress levels and surroundings will help you to become a more proactive, thoughtful and responsible handler.

Rest days may well be necessary for a dog prone to stress and anxiety, to allow the cortisol level to return to baseline. For a dog that becomes stressed on walks, a balance between exercise outside of the home and staying in to play, train and enjoy some quiet nap time will be needed. Other avenues to explore include looking into Sarah Fisher's ACE (Animal Centred Education) free work, Tellington TTouch Training, developing a sensory garden, having access to safe things to lick and chew on as part of their daily enrichment routine, and activities such as scentwork, which we will talk about in more detail in the final chapter.

In the case of a sound-sensitive dog, it is important to visit the vet so that pain can be ruled out, due to the link between sound sensitivity and pain; the comorbidity of sound sensitivity and separation anxiety should also be considered. If a dog is found to be suffering from an underlying condition such as Generalised Anxiety Disorder, it may well be that some medication might be necessary, alongside a behaviour modification plan. A dietary change might also be worth investigating with a nutritionist, as well as ensuring that the dog is getting enough sleep, regardless of his age. Whenever you see any change in behaviour, a vet visit should always be the very first step because of the correlation between pain and behaviour problems. Dr. Daniel Mills, FRCVS, a veterinary researcher and behaviourist at the University of Lincoln, states that approximately eighty percent of the behavioural issues that he sees in his own practice have a component of diagnosed or suspected pain.

Giving our dogs the option to make choices and never using force to coerce them will help to build their confidence and keep stress at bay. Always set them up to succeed and be sensitive to their needs so that they can build resilience, gain a sense of achievement and boost wellbeing. Walks should be a time for them to explore the sights, sounds and smells and be an enjoyable experience, so do allow them to take their time and sniff. Rather than setting a particular distance to walk, set a time goal and let them take the lead. In multi-dog households, set aside time for each dog to enable you to bond with each and fulfil their individual needs. Allow them time together if that's what they enjoy, but be mindful that they might also benefit from time apart. Be aware of your own state of mind when with your dog and consider what you might communicate to them and how that affects their emotional wellbeing.

A SUCCESS STORY TO LIGHTEN THE MOOD!

Pet name: Suzie
Racing name: Dixie Vixen
Date of birth: 18th March 2009
Sire: Brad The Lad, Dam: Speculation

Suzie's story began in Carlisle, Cumbria, and she now lives at the other end of the country in Rickmansworth, Hertfordshire. Suzie was one of a litter of nine and she loved her early life of running around the field with her siblings, full of confidence. When she finished her racing career, Suzie went to Sue at LTW and then on to Dogs Trust for re-homing, where was she was paired up with another Trailhound called Pat. Suzie and Pat became firm friends, remaining so to this day. Pat was re-homed, but as Suzie was a less confident hound, she was a little more difficult to re-home, and subsequently spent some time at the centre. Suzie really liked routine and had a small group of trusted people who cared for her and looked after her well, sometimes taking her home with them to give Suzie a break from kennels. Jo, Jan and Sandy would take Suzie for long walks in the local countryside with their own dogs, which included Pat who had been re-homed by Jo, who also had another Trailhound called Breeze. They all became good friends, and Jan and Jo remain an important part of Suzie's life today.

Mark and Spencer adopted Suzie in 2017, having admired her on the Dogs Trust website. The paperwork process was straightforward as they had adopted from Dogs Trust before. The centre's behaviourist explained that Suzie was anxious and worried around men and tried to deter Mark and Spencer, but they were certain that they wanted to meet her. Suzie was surprisingly relaxed around them and approached straight away (the sausages they had might have helped!). There were a further three visits a week for three weeks to ensure that this was a suitable match for everyone, all under the watchful eye of the Dogs Trust staff. The 4th March was re-homing day for Suzie, and she began her new life in Rickmansworth with Mark and Spencer.

Once settled in, it became apparent that Suzie's anxiety was affecting her quality of life. She was worried about lots of things, including flooring, walls, doorways, lights, stairs, loud noises, unknown people and dogs, wind, rain, shadows, and she toileted in her sleep. During Suzie's second week with them, Mark and Spencer had to resort to taking her into the vets in a wheelbarrow to avoid the flooring, which raised a lot of eyebrows! Physically, she was given a clean bill of health by the vet, but Mark and Spencer were advised to try Adaptil to see if it helped her anxiety; unfortunately, this did not work. The next option was Nutracalm, which gave her some relief for about a year, alongside training and much patience and dedication from Mark and Spencer. They really believed that the reason they were the ones to adopt Suzie was to help her overcome her anxiety; seeing even the tiniest amount of progress brought them overwhelming joy.

Mark and Spencer worked with the vet, Jo and Jan, the two volunteer walkers who remained in contact, and they gradually worked through Suzie's fears together. They went to a secure field together every weekend with all of the dogs, and Suzie gained confidence; she enjoyed life more and gained trust in people. Suzie would copy the other dogs and liked to dig a mud hole and then eat it! She would run off with the others, get stuck in dense thickets of brambles and have to be rescued regularly. Mark and Spencer soon learned that shorts were incompatible with Suzie! Suzie was doing so well that she went for a holiday with Jan one autumn, who sent Mark and Spencer videos of Suzie sunbathing happily in the garden, chasing around with Jan's dogs and dancing for her dinner! Suzie made herself at home and clearly felt very comfortable there, having a whale of a time.

After about a year, Suzie seemed to reach a bit of a plateau, so to help her progress further, she was prescribed Amitriptyline, an anti-depressant medication that is used, with some success, to treat chronic anxiety. She was slowly weaned off the Nutracalm so that she didn't become too drowsy from the combination of the two drugs, which might have made training more difficult.

Four years on, Suzie is far less anxious now and she enjoys learning new things. She is still quite wary of novel things and unfamiliar floors are still scary, so Mark and Spencer take some rolled up carpet for her if they go anywhere new, like royalty on the red carpet! She is now a much happier and far more relaxed hound who loves zoomies and being chased. Suzie shows Mark and Spencer that she wants to play by standing really still and giving them a cheeky sideways look for them to chase her until she wants them to stop!

Suzie

Suzie isn't meant to sit on the sofa unless invited, but she bends the rule by sprawling herself on top of Mark and Spencer and keeps one foot on the floor so she isn't fully on it. She loves to bark and howl for her dinner or a treat, and likes to rub her face and body on Mark and Spencer, enjoying a game of bitey-face with them (a bit too much!). Suzie enjoys sitting in wait for the postman and any unsuspecting joggers so that she can either chase them or stick her nose through the gate to say hello! Apart from sleeping and zooming, Suzie's favourite thing in the world is pizza. It has a magical power which turns Suzie into a very vocal, bouncy, confident girl, even before it's finished cooking. Suzie has pizza every Friday, without fail! Suzie feels safe enough to be curious because she has a loving family who won't make her do anything she doesn't want to, and she has comfy places to sleep whenever she likes; Suzie simply melts hearts wherever she goes.

Suzie

CHAPTER EIGHT

REACTIVITY: WHAT IS IT AND HOW DO WE MANAGE IT?

Reactivity is a term which I had not come across until about seven years ago. It is a fascinating subject which I have studied in great detail and feel passionately about due to it being a challenge faced by so many, but is so widely misunderstood. It is essential to learn what our dogs are communicating to us and understand how they might be feeling, so that we can avoid pressuring them by placing them in situations which might cause them stress. For those that have always had happy-go-lucky dogs which are phased by nothing, it is hard to appreciate the everyday difficulties faced by less confident dogs and their guardians, and the lengths we go to in order to make life as enjoyable and stress-free as possible. I think we have all fallen victim to a member of the "my dog is friendly" brigade at some point, being rudely interrupted by a loose dog with no recall, but for dogs that are a little less resilient, being approached by an off-lead dog can be a major incident which effects them for several days. It is really very difficult to understand the impact this can have until you have your own dog which displays reactive behaviours, but I hope this chapter will raise an awareness at least, and provide some insight into what reactivity is, what can cause it and how we can help our dogs.

Reactive behaviour in the domestic dog is classed as an overreaction to a certain stimulus or situation, from which it takes the dog some time to recover. Any reactive responses signify that there is an internal change in the state of the dog's nervous system and he is experiencing one of a range of emotions, including fear, anxiety, stress or frustration. He may have a single trigger, or stressors may be many and varied; it may be difficult to pinpoint what his trigger or triggers are if he does not respond consistently. He may appear to cope well with something one day but explode on another occasion, showing hugely varied behaviour depending on whether he is trigger stacked. Any reactive behaviour is not intended to embarrass or annoy their human, nor to make their life difficult, and it is not naughtiness. He is struggling in that moment; he feels threatened, and that he has no other option but to behave in this way.

The reactive dog may bark, lunge and growl and put on a show of threatening behaviour as a distance-increasing tactic, or conversely, he may run away to hide; survival is the aim, therefore fight isn't often a choice. The way a dog responds will vary from one dog to the next, depending on their physiology, past experiences, ability to cope, and their personality. The behaviour that we see is an attempt to deal with their stress and keep themselves safe.

FLOODING AND LEARNED HELPLESSNESS

It is important to note that not all overreactions will be overt, over-the-top ones. It is possible that a dog will not openly display his struggle, as seen in those who emotionally shut down. Just because a dog does not exhibit any obvious behaviours nor makes a lot of noise, it doesn't lessen what they are experiencing. They may feel unable to help themselves, therefore no longer try to do so, which is known as Learned Helplessness. Fully exposing our dogs to the things which frighten them is called Flooding, whether it is done deliberately or inadvertently, in a bid to help them overcome their fear. Flooding is a technique sometimes used in human exposure therapy, but it is a practice which the patient gives their consent for and fully understands what the process involves. However, when applied to dogs, who cannot give consent and have no understanding or rationale, it becomes extremely unethical. Instead of helping a dog overcome his fear, it will only compound it further by removing his choice to escape, and he will either fall into a state of learned helplessness, or he will opt for the fight response, in desperation. Despite the common belief that it will result in habituation, repeated exposure will not help a dog to become comfortable with something they fear; it will only sensitise him to it further and he will react increasingly to a specific stimulus, becoming more fearful.

SINGLE EVENT LEARNING

This leads on to another major consideration, something known as Single Event Learning, which can occur at any stage of a dog's life. One encounter resulting in a negative experience can trigger a fearful reaction and become ingrained in the memory, having a long-lasting impact. If it isn't addressed appropriately and carefully, it can lead to emotional shutdown, long-term fear, trauma, anxiety and phobias, therefore we must always respect how our dogs are feeling, regardless of whether we perceive their fear to be justified or rational.

Reactivity may start subtly, but as the dog rehearses these responses, the neural pathways strengthen, as does the behaviour. It is most commonly caused by a lack of proper and careful socialisation during critical growth periods, with genetics and any traumatic experiences that a dog may encounter also playing a part. There is also evidence to suggest that reactivity can be a learned behaviour from other dogs. Puppies learn through observing their Mum and interacting with their littermates; dogs which are new to the household may learn reactive behaviours from a dog that is already resident. It is also possible for us to reinforce reactive behaviours if we respond to our dogs inappropriately when they are scared, for example: laughing at a puppy running away from something they find scary can contribute to these behaviours becoming a habit.

SOCIALISATION

In terms of socialisation, the critical period for a puppy falls between the ages of six and fourteen weeks. Puppies need lots of positive experiences to shape how they view their world and everything within it. If new things are introduced pleasantly, allowing for happy memories and associations to develop, this will greatly reduce the likelihood of any future encounters being threatening to the puppy later on. If the puppy is not guided through this period, then negative associations may well form. This includes punishing any fearfulness, because scary or painful experiences will have long-lasting implications. Dogs will often present with undesirable behaviours to help them cope with a situation and if this is punished, it will cause further distress. If a puppy has no experiences at all, anything new will be potentially frightening for them. Dogs need to learn social skills in order to prevent everyday life from becoming stressful, with even the smallest of things causing anxiety.

SOCIAL DEVELOPMENT

Social development can be affected by a puppy being sent to a new home before the age of eight weeks old, because of missing out on important learning from his Mum and littermates. They will often have difficulty communicating with other dogs as a result, and will find it hard to build relationships and self-confidence, or learn how to problem-solve. These puppies can become destructive, with a tendency to be toy or food possessive, and are more likely to show fearfulness on walks, exhibit attention-seeking behaviours, suffer from noise reactivity, and bark excessively.

Dogs are very social animals and need company to be happy and healthy, and to prevent unwanted behaviours from arising. They are raised within a litter and once separated, they are entirely reliant on humans. Isolation can cause a lot of damage, particularly early on during the critical periods for socialisation. If isolated, they cannot learn good social skills and communication, nor practise different behaviours with feedback to help them learn. They won't be able to gauge whether they play too roughly and will not gain any experience of using calming signals or appeasement gestures, therefore they will be clueless how to behave appropriately in any given situation. This can lead to a lack of confidence, with fearful and reactive behaviours increasing.

Isolation can also lead to depression, which affects their appetite and ability to look after themselves. This can then lead to illness and disease, which becomes a vicious circle; the worse a dog feels, the less able he is to cope. Having high levels of stress has a direct impact on the immune system, which then makes illness even more likely. If the dog vocalises his distress but is ignored, this can be extremely traumatic, and if he is regularly left alone, he will soon learn to recognise pre-departure cues, which will heighten his levels of anxiety and cause emotional, mental and physical decline. This can lead to a variety of behavioural issues, including reactivity and aggression, or obsessive behaviours may develop to comfort themselves, such as tail, shadow, or reflection chasing. Tail chasing can morph into pulling at the hair, and an obsession can become so intense that the dog might no longer eat nor drink. If these behaviours become well-practised and deeply ingrained, they can be exceedingly difficult to overcome.

Another consideration is that puppies bought from pet shops are a lot more likely to exhibit poor behaviours, as demonstrated by a study carried out in 2011, led by Pierantoni. Breeding is an important factor, as genetics and DNA account for many inherited behaviours, besides environmental influences. There are inherited behaviour traits which can make reactivity more likely to surface, and they vary according to breed. Guardian breeds, such as the Pyrenean Shepherd, are naturally wary of strangers, and therefore more likely to be reactive to people than companion breeds that have been socialised and educated.

Stress during pregnancy can be transferred to unborn puppies, or if they witness reactive behaviours. Adrenaline and cortisol in increased levels affect neurons, which in turn affects the puppy's neural pathways and their ability to learn. This applies to puppy-farmed pups, as they spend several periods of critical development in a challenging environment. Dogs to be bred from are chosen with finances in mind rather than suitability of temperament, health or breed guidelines, which causes physical and psychological issues that are passed on to the litter. The dogs are often kept in extremely poor, isolated conditions, without proper care during the pregnancy, which then impacts on the puppies being carried. They miss out on the essential care and handling which they need early on, and many do not receive the very basics. No exposure to new experiences means they cannot develop their basic skills and are rarely handled. They have no freedom because of being caged, and there is no opportunity to learn and make positive associations, therefore paving the way for fear, anxiety, reactive behaviours and aggression. They cannot learn how to cope with day-to-day stressors, often being removed from their litter far too early and then being transported, perhaps to a new home, but some will find themselves in pet shops where they live a frustrating and stressful life. They are usually forced to eliminate in their living quarters, which hinders toilet training, besides causing them a good deal of stress. They are open to rough handling and being stared at by the public, so they are placed at a tremendous disadvantage, even prior to birth, and are likely to develop serious behavioural problems.

FEAR IMPRINT PERIODS

The way a puppy is handled during their first few days of living in a new home is crucial, as it is such a sensitive time for them. The puppy finds himself in a completely unfamiliar environment and is alone for the first time with new people, novel sights, sounds and smells, and he has no comfort or protection from his Mum or littermates. It is a scary time for them and they should have company during the day and at night time so that they are not left to cry, and they will need a lot of support so that a foundation of trust may be built. Puppies are very impressionable during developmental periods, with early experiences either giving confidence and building resilience, or they cause fearful behaviours which become permanent. The first fear imprint stage occurs between the ages of eight and eleven weeks old. During this time, any trauma can have far-reaching effects, as the puppy will associate anything connected to the trigger, such as sights, sounds and smells, with fear. Physical or psychological trauma during this period has been proven to cause avoidance behaviours.

The second fear imprint stage occurs between the ages of six and fourteen months old, and the puppy may appear to have ups and downs which correlate with growth spurts. Puppies can become frightened of something which didn't worry them previously, and they can become wary around new people and in new situations, so they require lots of support. As the puppy explores and gains independence, the flight instinct begins to develop, at about four months of age. They become increasingly self-aware, and scary situations become more likely to trigger a flight response as awareness of the need to survive develops. The hindbrain will activate during a scary experience and the puppy will seek to distance himself from the trigger, with no thought processes occurring. If the puppy is prevented from moving away or is verbally reprimanded or punished, the fear can become permanent. At about eight months of age there is a final physical growth stage, at which point puppies tend to enter a rebellious phase, often causing issues for new or inexperienced owners. This is a really crucial time in shaping the way in which the puppy enters adulthood; therefore, how the puppy's behaviour is handled will determine this. Behaviours may include experimenting and trying new things, perhaps regressing in toilet training, or mouthing and scent-marking may begin. New behaviours or old ones may surface. Owners can sometimes become exasperated and frustrated by their "failings" and may resort to harsh handling, which will then frighten the dog, spoiling the relationship and losing trust. This is often the reason that reactivity or aggression emerges. When dealing with puppy behaviours, it is important not to lose sight that it is a phase which the puppy needs guidance to pass through, and lots of patience is needed. Mental maturity often isn't reached until about eighteen months of age, and will vary depending on the breed.

Sometimes, an aggressive display may not be fear-based, but stems from frustration. There are dogs who we might class as "frustrated greeters" and react overtly on the lead, but usually settle once they are off-lead or can meet the approaching dog. Other dogs may be frustrated by not being able to gain access to another animal, such as a cat, or perhaps another person. Theses behaviours may begin fairly insignificantly because of their desire to interact. Although the underlying emotion is very different to fear-based reactivity, some of the same techniques used to change how they feel about other dogs can be employed, such as counterconditioning and desensitisation, helping them to learn some etiquette and calmness around others.

Having described what constitutes reactivity, some common responses and how reactivity can develop, I will look more closely at the effect upon a dog when he encounters something that frightens him. When faced with a trigger or new situation, the dog has a choice of either fight, flight, freeze, fool around, faint or fornicate. The response begins in the hypothalamus, which then reacts by regulating activity in the endocrine system, releasing hormones to alter the behaviour. Fight and flight are the most well known, but both would usually be a last resort. Freeze and faint result in the dog opting to stay still and hope for the best outcome, giving him the chance to evaluate the situation whilst not attracting any attention to himself. Faint is not a common response, but a pre-existing medical condition is usually a contributing factor. A freeze would indicate that the dog is over-threshold and needs distance from the trigger so that he can re-focus. Luring him with food will not work, as the fear response inhibits appetite and the digestive system. Not being able to take and eat food is an excellent indicator that the dog is feeling stressed. The longer the dog freezes for, the more likely he will be to escalate his behaviour, so it is important to move away from the trigger. In order to do this, massage or TTouch can help to relax his muscles enough to enable you to move him away calmly and slowly.

Fooling around is easily misinterpreted, as most people would assume that a wagging tail equates to a happy dog, but dogs overcompensate when they are feeling fearful. This can appear to be immature and inappropriate behaviour, but it is necessary to look at behaviours which are out of context and evaluate what is happening. If the dog is non-responsive to cues, it is likely that he is feeling under pressure. Flight responses include running or moving away from the trigger, and hiding behind the owner or any large objects in his environment. The fight response would normally be a last resort, but dogs tend to make themselves look threatening and imposing to scare off the trigger. They would usually try other options first, but if the trigger doesn't leave, they may feel forced to defend themselves.

Fear originates in the amygdala, the emotional centre, found in the temporal lobe. Whenever the dog shows interest in something, it is registered in the amygdala. A perceived threat triggers the release of stress hormones, activating the sympathetic nervous system, which is responsible for the fight-or-flight response. These hormones cause pupil dilation and increase breathing capacity, heart rate and blood pressure. Glucose is released to provide energy to enable the dog to escape, and the less important systems, such as digestion, shut down. These events happen subconsciously and are purely instinctive; no thinking occurs at all. The hippocampus, found in the prefrontal cortex, regulates the response, and this is where processing and interpretation takes place. It determines whether a threat is real, whether the response needs to continue, or if the parasympathetic nervous system can activate to relax the body. Occasionally, it is possible for the hippocampus and amygdala not to communicate properly, causing the response to stay activated. This causes several diseases and illnesses which manifest as a sudden onset of fear and anxiety.

AGGRESSION

In certain circumstances, aggression is a very natural behaviour, such as instinctive self-preservation. However, conflict and aggression that occurs regularly is not a well-balanced way of life for the dog. Aggressive responses can be triggered by something in the dog's external environment, or they can stem from a physiological change within the dog. There is some debate amongst experts over what constitutes aggression, with some including any level of barking, growling, snapping and lunging, whilst others classify aggression based solely on the intent of the dog. Reisner, a researcher, suggested in 1998 that "aggression is a harmful stimulus directed toward a subject, with evidence of intent and arousal, and toward which the target responds aversively." He excludes play but includes the "repertoire of postural threats preceding some bites". The clinical take on it, expressed by Beaver in 1999, is "…. one or more… distance-increasing behaviors….. expressed in an agonistic way as the dog asserted itself at the expense of someone else." He considers it a "threat of harmful behavior directed towards an individual".

(Above quotes taken from *responsibledog.net: Defining Canine Aggression By Joyce Kesling.*)

THE CANINE LADDER OF AGGRESSION

However, unlike reactive behaviours, there is a very clear progression and a different behaviour pattern, as outlined in the Canine Ladder of Aggression. This is a systematic escalation of warning signs that they feel uncomfortable, with many of the lower level signs appearing daily through the use of appeasement gestures. These gestures maintain peace and allow dogs to communicate how they are feeling. They can be used with other dogs as well as with humans, although we often do not recognise them for what they are. When the lower level signals are ignored, dogs learn to skip rungs on the ladder to make themselves understood. If any of their communications are punished or they can't move away, this can also lead to rungs being completely missed out. If breed-specific features or cosmetic alterations inhibit or prevent a certain display, they can learn that it is useless to try. Therefore, it is essential that we recognise and learn to accept the lower level signs/rungs so that we can diffuse the situation before the dog escalates.

Humans have very different ideas of what is socially acceptable than dogs do. Through observing a dog, we can usually gauge what is driving a behaviour, as there are many reasons aggression may occur, including pain, illness, medication, any changes within the body, genetically inherited aggression, fear, and conditioning. Much of what we would class as aggression is actually very normal, natural canine behaviour; they communicate through displays and vocalisation in order to avoid a fight from erupting. There are usually some very subtle, early indications of aggression that we do not recognise or overlook, such as our dog freezing over his food bowl or a bone as we walk past. He is displaying his discomfort caused by our proximity to him and his food, but we may be totally oblivious to this.

REACTIVITY OR AGGRESSION?

Reactivity is not the same as aggression, although it may appear so, as some responses can include aggressive ones. The aim of reactive behaviour is to increase distance between the dog and the trigger, whereas an aggressive dog actively seeks to decrease the distance. It is intention which separates the two: whether or not he is confrontational. Generally speaking, there are two types of aggression: fear-based non-confrontational aggression, and confrontational aggression, which means that they are willing to launch an attack. The fearful dog is unlikely to bite unless he cannot escape the trigger; he may cower, flash his teeth, growl and bark.

Any bites or snaps are likely to be quick and followed up with a retreat wherever possible. However, he may escalate straight to biting if he has learned that lower-level warnings go unheeded.

In contrast, confrontational aggression is not a fear-based behaviour. It may begin in this way, but the dog might have gained confidence by responding aggressively. The body language which accompanies confrontational aggression is quite specific: the dog's ears may go up and forwards, and he may give low and threatening vocalisations; there may be piloerection (raised hackles), assuming an intimidating stance with his body weight forwards, teeth on display, a direct stare, with a rigid body and tail. This differs from the reaction of a fearful dog, who will avert his eyes, turn the head or body away, or retreat from the trigger; he may freeze, lower the head or body, making himself appear smaller, with his ears pinned back. Again, there may be piloerection, growling and displaying of teeth. Any initial staring may morph into lunging and barking as a request to be left alone. If the dog's attempts for space are unsuccessful, he may then show aggression, and even bite as a last attempt to keep himself safe.

Sometimes, it is difficult to determine whether reactivity or aggression is at play, until the dog escalates his behaviour. There are many common denominators, such as showing his teeth, a stiffened body posture, and growling to show fear or anxiety, but when the dog closes his mouth, snaps, bites or muzzle punches, he has either been pushed right to his limits or his intentions are aggressive. However, a bite does not necessarily mean that the dog is aggressive; an aggressive rather than reactive dog can be driven by an element of fear.

When a dog engages in chasing, nipping at heels or jumping up in an attempt to bite, although this behaviour is present in some herding breeds, it is not a normal canine behaviour and needs to be treated as aggression. Some more overt signs which precede a bite include anxiety or arousal, direct eye contact which is maintained whilst showing the whites of the eyes, growling and a display of teeth, whereas the behaviour of a reactive dog is more erratic and may include spinning, lunging, jumping, pulling on the lead, barking, or trying to run away.

Some types of reactivity, such as barrier frustration, can lead to aggression if it isn't dealt with carefully early on, by changing the environment to prevent both the behaviour and the overarousal caused by that situation. The reactive dog will exhibit overarousal from either fear, frustration, or a lack of socialisation or training. He may be desperate to approach another dog but doesn't know how to express himself, or he may fear the other dog, or his human.

Aggression can fall into lots of different categories and is usually classified by what triggers it. There are usually other contributing factors and it is almost always rooted in fear, except for medical and health-related problems. Other causes include guarding territory, protective behaviours towards people, resource guarding, frustration, and prey-drive. Fear, frustration, pain and health issues can often play a part in both reactive and aggressive behaviours.

There are many forms of aggression and it is more important to find the triggers and cause, rather than to label the aggression. Learning what your dog's cues are and recognising when he is not comfortable is the first step in helping either the reactive or aggressive dog. Reactivity and aggression are similar in that both can be directed towards other dogs, people, objects or situations. At times, these behaviours are embarrassing, frustrating, sometimes scary and overwhelming, to the point where we feel that we have failed our dog, and the relationship becomes damaged.

Aggression is a serious issue and can arise in dogs who are mishandled, often by children. They are pushed past their ability to cope any longer and can be misunderstood. A previously well-balanced dog can eventually feel that he has no option but to react in an aggressive manner. This can become a coping mechanism over time, meaning that he may still choose aggression even when he has another choice. Equally, if the reactive dog's needs are not recognised and met, frustration can build and build, to the point

195

that reactivity turns into aggression. Chronic frustration can lead to feelings of anger, which can then develop into negative associations, causing the dog to respond aggressively. Reactivity should be addressed promptly to prevent this, because the dog will not grow out of it and it will not simply go away. Professional help and a positive behaviour modification plan will help to improve the reactivity and avoid it developing further towards aggression. Any sudden-onset aggression cases need to be taken for a veterinary examination as a matter of urgency, because of the correlation between behaviour changes and pain or illness.

MANAGING REACTIVE BEHAVIOUR

Whilst it is troublesome, a lot of reactive behaviour can be manageable with an understanding of arousal, triggers and trigger stacking, body language, counterconditioning and desensitisation, and the importance of space. However, attempting to treat aggression without a thorough understanding can worsen the situation and it is potentially very dangerous. Many dogs who are reactive do actually like other dogs, but they simply do not know how to behave around them. A dog that doesn't like other dogs, or has suffered a trauma from which he cannot recover, will resort to distance-increasing measures. Whether the cause of unwanted behaviours is reactivity or aggression, both conditions take time, patience, commitment, and often sacrifice, in order to help the dog.

There are lots of options for helping the reactive dog live a life as stress-free as possible but, ideally, we should be proactive from puppyhood. Early experiences shape who the puppy becomes in adulthood, so it is important to be cautious; but, that doesn't mean completely avoiding taking a puppy out or not letting him walk anywhere. Public areas where other pets may have been should not be accessed, but visits to family can be arranged. He can play in the garden and interact with trusted, suitable dogs, which will enable the puppy to have positive experiences. He needs opportunities to explore, experiment and practise normal everyday canine behaviours whilst being observed and kept safe. Taking these steps will ensure that the puppy learns how to communicate and read social cues, enabling him to navigate his way through life.

Any encounters with the puppy should be interactive; he should be observed, looking for signs of fear or concern, and we need to act accordingly. Socialisation is necessary in order to make happy memories and positive associations, so any outings need to be planned carefully, taking high-value treats each time and praising calmly. Taking the time to make car travel fun and safe will really help; treats and toys can be hidden in the car, leaving the doors open so that the puppy can explore without feeling trapped. Again, when meeting family, plan ahead and use toys and treats to make it a pleasant experience. Ensure that the puppy isn't bribed to approach, held longer than he is comfortable with, nor prevented from moving away; he should have the freedom to choose and to explore so that he can build confidence. Continuous positive socialisation and habituation throughout the dog's life is essential, particularly in the first few years, and throughout all learning and developmental stages.

Once a dog begins to exhibit reactivity, we need to address this as soon as possible so that these behaviours do not become practised and ingrained. Once we have identified what the dog's trigger or triggers are, we should not force him out of his comfort zone in an attempt to get him to confront his fear. If he is placed in this position, he will be forced to escalate to scare the trigger away, thus reinforcing the behaviour. It will become a learned behaviour and he will use the tried and tested method that works for him. Punishment must not be used because the dog will associate the trigger with fear and pain; it is not possible to punish fear out of a dog, it will only worsen the problem.

When addressing the dog's fears, we need to discover what his flight distance is so that we can work with him below his stress threshold. Flight distance will vary for every dog; some may cope fairly well within a certain distance from a trigger, whereas another might not cope at all. The dog should always have the choice to move away from a trigger, otherwise we risk triggering fear-aggression if the dog feels trapped. Being on-lead removes this choice, so we should be mindful and allow him as much distance as he needs to feel safe. We need to try to understand what the dog is feeling, rather than attempt to suppress the unwanted behaviours that we see.

When working with the reactive dog, he should not be placed in situations where he feels the need to escalate. We need to be observant, looking for any early signs of stress, taking action before he goes beyond his threshold, and we need a good understanding of canine body language and what the dog is communicating to us. When he can work at his own pace, a trusting relationship with his human will develop and he will gain confidence. It is possible to overcome the fear, but it takes time and patience. Take the pressure off, allow him to explore, and he will succeed through positive experiences, mental stimulation, and boundaries. He will need reassurance, and not be ignored or reprimanded. It is a common misconception that you can reinforce fear by providing comfort during fearful moments, but that is not the case. Forcing a dog to face his fear or ignoring his efforts to communicate will undermine your relationship and his trust in you, which can lead to emotional shutdown and learned helplessness. He may give up completely and he will take a long time to recover from this state.

Other things to consider include the equipment that the dog wears when being exercised. A well-fitting Y-shaped harness with two points of contact and a double-ended lead will usually be the best option, rather than a collar and lead. If a reactive dog pulls or lunges, it can be very damaging to the delicate neck area, plus the sensation of the oxygen restriction can also heighten their sense of panic. There are various lead handling techniques, such as the TTouch lead stroke, which can be beneficial if a dog freezes, and it is important not to put tension through the lead, which will communicate your anxiety to the dog. It is much easier to focus on and manage your reactive dog when he is walked alone, as every dog has their own individual needs and difficulties. It is worth finding the time to do this if you have a multi-dog household.

There are lots of behaviours which we can teach our dogs to help them cope better, such as "middle," "behind," counting games to build focus, and a U-turn when we need to move them away quickly. We can introduce scatter feeding at home and when on walks, which comes in handy if the dog is a little too aroused to take food from your hand but can eat it from the ground. Sniffing for the food is relaxing for them, but it also offers a calm behaviour display to another dog in the vicinity. However, it is best avoided if the unknown dog is off-lead, as they may come and investigate for some food of their own, or worse, they may be food-aggressive. Other tactics include using objects in the environment as a barrier, such as a fence, a wall, or a car, to make them feel safer.

Carefully planned meetings with a stooge dog can provide a suitable setting for practising social skills at a safe distance, including approaching on a wide arc, walking parallel and taking it in turns to go in front, all with no face-to-face interactions. Having the chance to let off steam in a secure field and have a good run is beneficial for all because the humans can relax with their dogs and enjoy simply being together, without the worry of the possibility of meeting any potential triggers. The mindset of the human is equally important as the dog's because if we are anxious, this will transfer to the dog and could exacerbate the situation; decompression walks are excellent for everyone, for this reason.

Living with a reactive dog can certainly feel like a bit of an emotional roller-coaster, and can be quite traumatic for both the human and their dog. However, with the right management tools in place, a behaviour modification plan, and lots of time, patience and understanding, it is possible to change the situation for the better. Although it is tempting to wonder what it must be like to have a "normal" dog that you can take anywhere and do anything with, there is so much more to a reactive dog than just the label, and their reactivity does not define who they are. We all have challenges to face and, although it can be a long process to work through reactivity, it is important to celebrate even the smallest of successes, as they all contribute towards a calmer, happier, and more peaceful way of life for the dog and his human family.

In the next chapter I will discuss counterconditioning and systematic desensitisation in detail, because it forms an essential part of any behaviour modification plan. The principle of pairing high-value food with a trigger and gradually decreasing distance over time is fairly straightforward, but being able to effectively and successfully put it into practice is far from easy. This is not helped by the fact that there is a huge misunderstanding, even amongst a good deal of canine professionals, of what counterconditioning entails and how to perform it correctly, so it is very difficult to find the right information and guidance. Getting to grips with the timing of the food delivery can be a challenge, as well as overcoming one of the biggest hurdles, the use of the word "reward". This implies that the dog is expected to offer a behaviour in return for the food, which is not the case at all. We are purely pairing the presence of a trigger with something that the dog values highly in order to change how he feels about it, creating a positive conditioned emotional response. Teaching behaviours, known as operant conditioning, can be introduced later to provide the dog with further coping strategies, but to perform counterconditioning correctly we must move away from the idea of behaviour and reward and realise that we are working on an emotional level.

CHAPTER NINE

COUNTERCONDITIONING AND DESENSITISATION

When working with a fearful dog, it is important to first build confidence and trust. Having environmental management in place, along with any necessary medications, will help to support the dog whilst working through a behaviour modification plan. If the dog can develop a strong relationship with the handler first, it will help him engage and focus and he will be better able to cope when training around triggers. A thorough vet check is also essential in order to rule out any physical causes, because of the strong correlation between pain and behavioural issues.

Once a fearful response has already been established, it is crucial that the emotions driving the reactive behaviour are addressed, rather than tackling the behaviour through operant conditioning only (teaching and asking for behaviours). When the focus is placed upon addressing the cause of the fear, then the unwanted behaviours will resolve rather than being suppressed, and will be far more effective in improving behaviour and confidence in the long term. When we understand that these behaviours are driven by an emotional response and are fear-based, it is clear that any aversive methods employed will only further complicate the problem by adding to the fears of the dog, therefore damaging the trust and bond between dog and handler in the process.

Before embarking on a behaviour modification plan, the level and type of exercise which the dog receives, both mental and physical, should be assessed. He needs to be able to run and burn off excess energy, and play and interact with other dogs (if access to other dogs is appropriate for that particular dog). He will need sufficient human input with training, brain games and interaction to teach him how to learn and to give him purpose, rather than just being left to amuse himself in the garden. Through training, the dog can be taught cues which will help to build a language connection and strengthen the bond between dog and handler.

The structure within the household will need to be assessed because routine and consistency are both vital, along with positive teaching and clear, fair boundaries to set him up to succeed. The dog's diet should also be considered and examined to ensure that it is healthy and balanced, and he needs constant access to clean, fresh water. Diet has an enormous impact on behaviour, so he will need proper nutrition to support a positive behaviour modification plan.

A dog that finds himself in a stressful situation will escalate to survival mode if he feels he is in danger. Past experiences, learning, his state of health, genetics, temperament, and ability to escape, will all determine whether he opts for fight or flight, or waits to see what will transpire. Most will choose flight in order to avoid any conflict and ensure their survival, whilst the fight response occurs when a dog feels unable to escape. These encounters cause the dog to become chemically altered, and frequent exposure will lead to physical and mental damage, including chronic stress. This will begin to destroy the immune system and will seriously affect the dog's ability to learn; it can also create hypervigilance and reduces the dog's capacity to relate to their environment. Eventually, it will decimate their quality of life and it will take a very long time for them to return to a healthy body chemistry and mental state. Therefore, it is essential that management is in place to minimise exposure as much as possible outside of training sessions, and to prevent the dog from becoming overwhelmed and flooded.

Any reactive behaviours which become deeply ingrained are very difficult to overcome, although not impossible, through the use of counterconditioning and careful systematic desensitisation. Although they are two separate principles, they are most successful when used together. Basically speaking, counterconditioning is used to change the current negative feelings attached to a trigger to positive feelings. This is a deep-rooted, non-conscious response towards a stimulus, whether that is another dog, person, object, environment or an event; these feelings are beyond the control of the dog. Systematic desensitisation means carefully controlling the distance between the dog and the trigger, whilst gradually reducing the proximity to build tolerance to it, always staying below the dog's threshold. By carefully combining the two, tolerance can be increased without negatively affecting their emotional and physical wellbeing. A consistent positive conditioned emotional response at each stage of decreasing the distance, whilst working sub-threshold, is essential. Every dog is an individual, so it is impossible to set a time frame for the process. The handler should not feel discouraged as time goes on; every little success, however small, deserves to be celebrated! Training should be carefully balanced with respite time to allow the dog to recuperate and decompress.

Although very time-consuming, counterconditioning is a fairly straightforward and highly effective process, once it is fully understood. It builds new neural pathways, creating a positive emotional response to something that has previously held a negative association for the dog by pairing it with something pleasant, such as high-value treats or a toy, whichever the dog favours. Through the use of positive reinforcement we can activate a release of dopamine, the main neurotransmitter associated with memory. Dopamine is triggered by a positive environmental circumstance and is the key to the brain's reward system. It boosts learning, builds motivation, increases focus and attention and the capacity for clear thought, and it boosts motor skills. The good feelings triggered by it are stored in the memory, therefore it is vital in creating a positive conditioned emotional response.

A common misconception of counterconditioning is that you are rewarding "bad" behaviour by feeding treats, but we are purely working on an emotional level to change how the dog feels. Counterconditioning is particularly effective because it doesn't involve asking anything of the dog; it can be carried out with no focus on the handler at all, and only requires the dog to be at a neutral level of exposure to facilitate it. The handler doesn't even need to know why the dog may feel negatively about a particular trigger in order to help him. Counterconditioning can be used in lots of situations for a variety of fears, such as household appliances, vehicles, people and dogs.

It is important to control the environment carefully, work at the dog's pace, and ensure sessions always remain positive to maintain confidence levels. Sometimes it may be necessary to abandon a session if it becomes apparent that the dog might be struggling with the effects of trigger stacking, or if something takes the dog by surprise whilst actively training. Times like these often need quick thinking and a really well practised "let's go" cue to make a hasty exit. Other tactics to incorporate into your training are sprinkling treats on the ground for your dog to snuffle for while a trigger passes by, and using physical barriers in the environment to retreat behind in order to avoid a reaction and a negative encounter. If a dog goes beyond his coping threshold, he will learn nothing because the stress response has been activated and he cannot think clearly, therefore forging ahead with the session will be counterproductive.

To explain further, let's take the scenario of a dog that is fearful of other dogs he sees whilst on walks. Before tackling this, all training sessions should be well planned, with much consideration given to the location, how much space is available, the frequency that dog walkers will pass by, as well as minimising the potential for the session being interrupted by off lead dogs running up or other triggers appearing, such as bikes or children. Apart from increasing the likelihood of a reaction, which will jeopardise your training, it is also a factor in how classical conditioning functions. A dog may well have multiple triggers, but in order to fulfil the 1:1 contingency that is necessary when counterconditioning, triggers will need to be identified, prioritised, and then worked on one at a time.

As an example, let's say that the high-value treat being used is hotdog sausages. When the trigger appears at a safe distance and the dog has definitely seen it, hotdog sausage is fed continuously until the trigger is no longer in sight. The sausage can only be fed in this situation so that the dog can make the association that the trigger appearing always means hotdogs; he should not be fed hotdogs at any other time. It is also important that the food used is actually high value for the dog and not just something that the handler has selected; offering the dog a variety of foods and watching to see which he shows most interest in is a good way to determine this. Dealing with reactivity is an immense challenge, so it is imperative that the reinforcement matches the task at hand.

While the delivery of high-value food needs to meet the 1:1 contingency for the appearance of other dogs to always predict hotdogs, every other possible variable also needs to be managed in order to prevent other associations from being formed. Apart from the link between the food and the trigger, nothing else should be predictable about the training sessions. This means training at different times of day, in different locations with different length training sessions, as well as varying the preparation routine of getting ready to leave and varying how, when and where the trigger appears.

There are a few points which should be established before training commences. These include: the distance from the trigger at which the dog can remain calm, the length of exposure the dog is able to tolerate before showing signs of stress, how the dog responds to the trigger when both moving and stationary, and if there is a change in intensity to his reaction depending on colour variation, breed, size and shape. The starting distance should be such that the dog is aware of the trigger but remains well below his threshold, showing no signs of unease. The dog should consistently be relaxed in the presence of the trigger before moving any closer, to ensure that his wellbeing is protected and progress isn't compromised.

In terms of location, a good starting point is a public area where dogs will be kept on the lead and where there will be a steady flow of dog walkers. This could be somewhere in view of a footpath which crosses a recreation ground, for example, where the handler can position the dog at a safe distance, hopefully with a fence behind in order to ensure they are protected from an approach from the rear.

When counterconditioning, it is important to wait until the dog has seen the trigger before feeding, to ensure that the trigger predicts the treats and not the other way around. If the food appears before the trigger, the food can become "poisoned" by creating a negative association with the food, because the food will become a predictor of the scary thing. If this happens, the handler should stop using that particular food, find a suitable replacement, and start again. There is no need to point out the trigger to the dog either; he should be allowed to notice it and look at it in his own time. There is a chance that pointing out triggers to the dog could lead to hypervigilance, as well as further fear and panic. Once the dog has seen the trigger, the handler should start dispensing food. If the dog cannot take the treats, grabs at them or uses his teeth more than usual, this indicates overarousal and he needs the handler to increase distance from the trigger. The handler should continue to feed until the trigger is no longer present, always maintaining distance so that the dog remains below threshold.

If a dog is only reactive to certain others, it would be beneficial to carry out counterconditioning every time a dog is encountered in order to consolidate the association between the food and other dogs; it will help to build a bank of pleasant experiences and associations. Over time, and if carried out correctly, the dog will see the trigger and will associate it with food and pleasant feelings, automatically checking in with the handler in anticipation of the treats. At this stage, they will demonstrate relaxed, happy and soft body language. This means that a positive conditioned emotional response is forming and once it is consistent, the next step is to start work on the desensitisation aspect.

Desensitisation comes into play once a consistent positive conditioned emotional response has been established. The handler has reached the point of being able to move closer to a trigger by exposing the dog at a safe level, reducing the size of the dog's safety bubble gradually, while increasing his ability to cope with things in his immediate environment. It is crucial that the handler does not rush this process, therefore flooding the dog. This is a very outdated method based on forcing the dog to face his fear and continuing to expose him until he no longer reacts; it is both unethical and hugely detrimental to the dog. It is potentially dangerous, as fear can quickly escalate to aggression, but it can also cause irreparable damage emotionally and physically, sadly often leading to emotional shutdown and learned helplessness. Unfortunately, an absence of behaviour can be misinterpreted to mean that the dog is coping, therefore employing the help of a good, qualified professional is often the best course of action. This will allow the dog to be carefully monitored for the earliest signs of stress, it will ensure that he is coping, and will facilitate progress being made.

To counter-condition a trigger such as a vacuum cleaner, a similar process needs to be followed. There are several factors to consider, such as the noise, the movement, and you interacting with it, so start with it present in the room but not switched on. Leave the door open and ensure that there is a clear escape route so that the dog does not feel trapped and is free to leave at any time. Do not encourage or force any interaction through luring or bribery, as the dog may feel conflicted between wanting the food and how scary he finds the vacuum cleaner.

When the dog looks at the vacuum, (we need the dog to see the trigger), feed him treats and continue to give them while he remains in the vicinity. When he is comfortable with this, and only then, progress to standing near the vacuum, perhaps with your hand resting on it, and then repeat the process as before. You may need to throw the treats away from you and the vacuum so that he does not have to approach to receive the treats. Once your dog is at ease with this stage, progress to moving it very slowly, being careful not to make any erratic movements which might frighten the dog. When he is comfortable with these steps, progress to having it stationary and switched on, building back up to you pushing it. Once he is happy with the entire process, continue to carry treats and feed him as you vacuum so that you can reinforce his learning and the positive association that he now has between the vacuum and the food.

Counterconditioning can be used in lots of situations for a variety of fears, such as other household appliances, vehicles, people and dogs. It is important to control the environment, work at the dog's pace, and keep sessions short and positive.

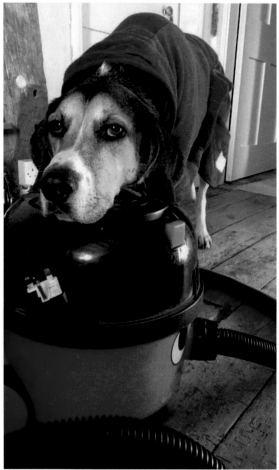
Michele Smith's Paddy

For a storm-phobic dog, a CD recording of storm sounds may help to desensitise him gradually. Begin by playing the sounds at a very low level, pairing them with high-value food. Once the dog is consistently relaxed, very slowly increase the volume, ensuring there are no signs of stress at each incremental level.

Helen Parish's Jelly and Nutkin

This probably will not resolve the dog's fear completely, because there are lots of factors at play during a storm which the dog may react to, such as the barometric pressure, any static in the air, light flashes from lightning, and any accompanying smells. All may well be contributing factors to the dog's fear, and the CD will only be able to address the sound element of the storm; medication may well be needed in order to provide the right level of support for the dog. Fireworks might also be challenging to counter-condition, so it is important to create a safe space for your dog, muffling as much of the sound as possible by using appliances such as a radio, tv, fans, or a white noise machine; lower-pitched frequencies will mask the booms better. The curtains will need to be drawn and any views to outside shielded so that any flashes of light do not frighten the dog.

For a dog suffering with separation anxiety, it is possible to desensitise him to the pre-departure cues which trigger the panic. Dogs watch us constantly, particularly those that are anxious, and they are able to chain together lots of actions so that the very first thing that you do to get ready to leave, probably subconsciously, can communicate your intention to leave and trigger the anxious behaviour. First, you will need to work out what the dog's "baseline" is; in other words, what his threshold is for being alone before he shows any signs of stress. This is best carried out through videoing your dog, to allow for accurate monitoring and assessment. The baseline test should be done without the aid of a KONG or licki-mat etc, as food may distract the dog temporarily until it runs out, and anxiety or panic might then set in.

Although a loss of appetite is a common symptom of stress, some dogs may express their stress through over-eating. They need to learn to be comfortable, with no added distractions which may mask their anxiety for a short period. All training needs to be carried out below the dog's coping threshold for it to be successful. When working through separation anxiety, you need to make a commitment to not leaving your dog alone, except during the very brief training periods. This might mean asking a family member to sit with him, doggie day care visits, day-boarding at kennels, or perhaps working from home. The amount of time that he can manage alone may be zero to start with, or it may be a few minutes.

When beginning the desensitisation, you will need to work on exercises such as the "flitting game," developed by Emma Judson, where you move between two rooms frequently for short periods, so that your dog becomes less interested in following, is slower to get up, and eventually learns to settle. The "door is a bore" game works similarly, involving lots of work on opening and shutting the door until the dog no longer associates this with being left. Other pre-departure cues can be gradually added in during the course of the training. It is always best to work with a qualified professional because separation anxiety is extremely distressing for all involved, due to the nature of this panic disorder. It takes a lot of time and an enormous amount of commitment to work through successfully, so the moral support and guidance that a professional can provide really will be invaluable.

In order to provide a solid basis for the counterconditioning and desensitisation process, lots of time and patience will be needed, along with a protective environment and a good diet. When working with a scared dog, carefully observing his body language and evaluating what he is communicating will help to maintain his self-esteem, along with always giving him the space he needs. Provide him with opportunities to make choices and do not force him into potentially uncomfortable situations; minimise exposure to triggers to reduce stress and always monitor carefully.

Fear and reactivity result from a lack of knowledge, as the dog has not learned how to cope in certain situations. This may be because of a lack of exposure, perhaps he was never taught how to cope, or it may be a learned behaviour. We need to protect our dogs and take responsibility for teaching them what they need to live alongside us, rewarding them and teaching alternative behaviours instead of punishing the less desirable ones. Fear and reactivity result from the survival response. The dog does not enjoy feeling this way; he is really struggling. It is not his fault, either. He is not misbehaving nor deliberately giving us a hard time, but needs help and guidance, rather than being made to feel worse. Time, patience and understanding are needed, along with the skills to carry out counterconditioning and desensitisation successfully, to treat the fears that our dogs live with.

Having discussed canine stress, reactivity, training and management strategies that we can put in place to help our dogs deal with everyday life more easily, it is time to move on to another passion of mine: the canine nose and scentwork! In the next chapter you will find guidance on how to introduce, provide and incorporate enrichment and scentwork into your dog's life, regardless of their age, breed, or physical capabilities. Both are an excellent way to build confidence and resilience, as well as being hugely enjoyable! Scentwork can be trained for fun or for competition, and is a wonderful way to develop the bond between you and your dog; it relies very much on you working as a team.

The canine nose is absolutely phenomenal, and I never cease to be amazed by what they can achieve and are capable of. Mental stimulation is just as vital as physical exercise, and a daily dose of enrichment and scentwork will help to fulfil that requirement, whilst making your dog a very happy pooch!

Helen and Dave Warrington's Ali

CHAPTER TEN

THE CANINE NOSE

The dog's senses are the link between the world and his brain: the eyes, ears, sense of touch and taste are all direct routes to it. The brain is the memory storage area, leading to the ability to learn to search for a specific item, and to remember previous lessons on scent and technique. The dog's sense of smell is the key way in which he views the world, in contrast with humans who see the world through their eyes, primarily. To emphasise the importance of this sense, it is worth noting that when puppies are born, they have a heat-seeking capability through their noses, which helps them to orientate towards their Mum and the rest of the litter. They are born unable to see, and their hearing is not yet developed. Therefore, the nose is of vital importance, particularly as it takes a few days for the eyes and ear canals to open.

The dog's sense of smell is so refined that he can distinguish gender, health, illness, what the weather is, what time of day it is, what was eaten the day before, the need to toilet, and our own unique and distinct scent. They communicate socially by scent, not just through body language such as calming signals, appeasement gestures and displacement behaviours. The average dog has two hundred and twenty million olfactory receptors in the nose, although it can be as many as three hundred million in dogs bred specifically for scentwork, who tend to have longer ears which help to capture the scent and move it towards the nose. In comparison, the human has an average of only six million scent receptors.

Michele Smith's Paddy

Dogs detect scent through the tiny particles that surround an item as it moves through the air, via the process of diffusion. The way in which scent diffuses varies widely, with gas and vapour having the strongest scent and solids having the weakest, because the particles are more tightly knitted together. When a dog is searching for an item, they follow the increasing level of scent until they reach the item. The smellier an object is, the more easily the dog will find it. The odour forms a scent pool, which is the density of the scent as it diffuses away from an item. With no movement in the air, the scent will be diffused evenly around the object, forming a pool effect. If there is air movement, the scent particles will form a cone shape in the direction that the air is moving. The dog then follows the pool or cone shape of the scent density to reach the search item or object. The scent particles pass through softer materials quicker than solid ones, so will result in a different scent picture for the dog. With larger obstacles, scent tends to bounce off them and back again, resulting in a mix of high-density scent particles.

Air temperature also affects how the dog detects scent. When it is warmer, the scent particles enlarge and rise, so they may be detected above the dog's head. When it is colder, the scent particles will shrink and remain closer to the ground. When a dog is scenting, the outer parts of the nostrils move to allow for expansion and contraction, preventing the entry of foreign bodies. He will often close his mouth when he finds a trace of a scent, to allow more air to pass into the nasal cavity.

The canine frontal cortex is smaller than our own, therefore it has different emotional capabilities; it is this part of the brain that is responsible for conscious scent perception. When it comes to canine scenting ability, their brains are forty times more capable than our own. When a dog is sniffing, he inhales the scent into his nasal cavities, where the particles are caught in mucus and then processed by the sensory cells. The soft tissue inside the nasal area accommodates both air and scent, but can still differentiate between the two. Scent and air are separated in the nasal cavity immediately after inhalation. Air is filtered to the lungs and circulatory system to carry oxygen to the cells, while scent travels upwards to the olfactory receptors and olfactory bulb at the front of the brain. The smaller quantity of air arrives here, where turbinates, which are small, bony structures, "strain" the scent, which then triggers the dog's olfactory receptors to connect with the brain and process the scent. Exhalation occurs through the slits at the side of the dog's nose to prevent scent from being expelled from the nostrils; the dog can draw in fresh scents continuously and breathe out old ones. They can also determine which scents entered through which nostril!

Approximately a third of the brain is dedicated to the ability to detect scent. Scent receptors extend on cilia (hair-like receptor cells) from each of the sensory cells into the nasal cavity; the scent receptors trap the smells, and the messages are delivered via sensory axons (transmission lines) to the olfactory bulb. Once here, scents are carried to the frontal cortex as well as to other regions of the brain, including the centres for emotions, memory and pleasure. These are all interconnected, which helps the dog to translate the meaning of the smells. The scent arrives at the hippocampus for scent recognition, whilst the hypothalamus and amygdala deal with the emotional and motivational aspects. The olfactory cortex then distinguishes whether the scent is known or a new one, and then distributes it to the relevant area of the brain.

The Jacobson's organ, also known as the vomeronasal organ, forms the secondary olfactory system and has a primary function of detecting pheromones and the opportunity to breed. It is found inside the nasal cavity and opens into the top part of the mouth and at the base of the nasal passage. The Jacobson's organ does not detect ordinary odours, but responds to substances with large molecules, which are often odourless. The sensory cells communicate with the accessory bulbs and the reproductive and emotional part of the brain. The pheromone processing and interpretation is kept separate from that of basic odours, as the Jacobson's organ has its own set of nerves leading to the pheromone-analysing part of the brain. The canine nose and sense of smell are hugely expanded by the Jacobson's organ, and certain scents may well be linked with memories and emotions.

PROVIDING ENRICHMENT
THROUGH SCENTWORK

Dogs use their noses to interpret their environment and love to sniff and forage. Scentwork encourages natural behaviours and helps to build confidence, resilience, and understanding. It provides mental stimulation whilst giving them a job to do and builds a trusting bond between dog and handler. Scentwork can be engaged in by dogs of any age or breed to keep them physically and mentally active, even by those recovering from injury, illness, or on restricted exercise. If there simply isn't much space, it can be practised both indoors and outdoors. Searching is more intense than sniffing alone and is hugely rewarding. Because of the way in which a partnership of trust and communication forms between dog and handler as they work together, it can even help highly reactive dogs. When dogs are scenting, searching or foraging, the action of sniffing while processing oxygen and scent simultaneously has a relaxing effect, lowering the pulse rate and using a lot of energy, which is why ten minutes of scentwork equates to about an hour of physical exercise. The more intense the sniffing, the greater the benefit to the dog. The study can be found here: www.dogfieldstudy.com

To counteract raised arousal levels from physical exercise and any trigger stacking, the adopter will need to include activities which will help to empty the dog's stress bucket and boost relaxation. In addition, an outlet for stress and prevention of boredom is needed to support the dog in being able to express normal canine behaviours. Problem solving with food is an excellent way to do this, particularly for nervous dogs, as no human contact is necessary. Introducing some games will help hugely in building confidence and self-belief, as long as it isn't used to lure the dog; this can lead to approach avoidance conflict and a fear of hands.

Watching how our dogs tackle these tasks teaches us a lot about their current levels of confidence, optimism and resilience. Anything which involves sniffing will be of enormous benefit as it is mentally and physically tiring, as well as extremely fulfilling for the dog. Scatter feeding smelly foods such as finely chopped liver or grated cheese outdoors on short grass is a great way to start, or if the dog isn't yet able to cope with being outdoors, an alternative is a towel folded in half with treats placed in the middle. Using high-value treats will motivate the dog and provide a two-fold reward alongside the positive feelings from his success.

Food is a primary reinforcer and triggers dopamine, providing a memory and motivation boost whilst also satisfying foraging, scavenging and hunting needs too. Toys can be used to boost dopamine, but not all dogs love toys, nor indeed will have experience of them or know how to play with them. The adopter should sit and watch from a distance, looking toward the dog rather than directly at him. As he gains confidence over time, the activities can gradually increase in difficulty. Snuffle mats, items with pockets, odd socks, licki-mats, Kongs etc can be included as part of the daily routine; any household items such as recycling materials can also be used for enrichment, as long as they are safe, not posing a choke hazard.

My own hounds really enjoy a "busy box," which is an empty cardboard box with toilet roll tubes in which I hide treats, and then seal the ends with paper. To make it more challenging, I sometimes wrap the treats as well, and add extra shredded paper to the box. They absolutely love foraging and ripping up the cardboard, and I have taught my more confident dog to tidy up, picking up all the rubbish and putting it in the empty box for more treats! However, it is important to start at a simple level and not add any pressure, so that the dog can succeed and build confidence in making choices. The adopter should watch to see how their dog approaches the tasks and provide some gentle vocal encouragement, if that is appropriate for the individual dog.

To ensure that the activity is enriching, the dog should not be hungry; he should be observed to ensure that frustration does not creep in and that he does not lose confidence at any point. Environmental enrichment is a fantastic way to enhance a dog's life and will provide entertainment for both the dog and the adopter, as well as being empowering for the dog. It can be a great confidence booster if managed carefully; enrichment which promotes trying new things and uses the brain to problem solve builds resilience, and can provide much-needed respite for anxious or fearful dogs.

The following is a step by step, easy to follow training plan which I put together, and I wanted to share it because I know that many people struggle with where to start and how to introduce enrichment and scentwork. It is something which all dogs should have access to and be able to enjoy, but I feel it is particularly important for our Trailhounds, bearing in mind their previous lives and what they have been so carefully bred to do. My training plan can be adapted to suit any dog, and it covers all the stages of searching an area, assuming that the dog has no search training at all. The focus of the plan is fun and life enrichment.

12 STEP TRAINING PLAN

STAGE 1: SCATTER FEEDING

Goals:
- The dog can spend ten minutes happily searching for food scattered or hidden in both indoor and outdoor areas, at different heights.
- To introduce the search cue to the dog.

You will need:
- Small, smelly, tasty, high-value treats.
- A low-distraction area to train in.
- Choose what your search cue will be, such as "find it."

Steps:

Starting in a small, low-distraction area, drop a handful of treats for the dog to sniff out and eat. As the dog gains confidence, scatter the treats more widely. To gradually increase the difficulty, start to vary the location, distraction level and the height that you place the food, and begin to hide it rather than scatter. Always observe the dog to ensure that he is enjoying the activity and to safeguard his confidence.

In order to introduce a cue to search, use your chosen cue word as you release your dog to sniff out the food; he will soon catch on! Scatter feeding is a great way to help your dog to relax, and for a dog that tends to eat quickly from a bowl, it is a handy activity to slow him down at mealtimes. Start to integrate this activity into daily life for your dog.

STAGE 2: INTRODUCING A MARKER

Goals:
- To "power up" the chosen marker so that the dog clearly identifies the marker with a reward.
- To build your own confidence in using a marker.
- To "dial up the dopamine" whilst establishing calmness to enhance learning.

You will need:
- Lots of tiny, high-value treats that can be easily swallowed without chewing.
- Decide what the marker will be, whether that is a clicker or a word such as "nice" (the dog will process a click quicker than a word, therefore allowing for more accurate marking.) If the dog is deaf, a visual marker can be used, such as a "thumbs up" or a flashlight.
- A low-distraction area to train in.

Steps:
Wait for a calm moment, deliver your chosen marker to the dog and reward immediately. Follow the pattern "mark and treat, wait a beat" (this will ensure that the marker predicts the food). Repeat this for up to five minutes at a time, with several sessions of this per day for several days, or until the connection is made.

Troubleshooting:
If the dog becomes over-aroused, wait for him to pause and then mark and reward. Remember that our actions influence the dog, so stay calm and move slowly. If the dog grabs at the food, put it into a closed hand; wait for calmness before offering the food. This will teach him that polite behaviour earns him the reward.

If you have a sound-sensitive dog and you are using a clicker, be aware that the clicker may startle them; you could wrap it in a towel to muffle it until they have a positive conditioned emotional response to the sound.

How do we know that the dog has made the connection between the marker and reward? Test the marker. Wait for a calm moment, mark, and observe the dog's reaction. If he looks for his treat, then the marker is "powered up". **Remember: always reward after a marker to maintain its power, even if the marker is mis-timed or used by mistake.**

STAGE 3: INTRODUCING FREE SHAPING

Goals:
- To teach the dog that when he offers a desirable behaviour, the marker will be delivered and he will receive a reward.
- To develop his thinking ability.
- To lay the foundations for shaping a particular behaviour.
- To improve accuracy in your use and timing of the marker.

You will need:

- An empty cardboard box of a suitable size for the dog (low enough to step into and large enough to accommodate the dog if he chooses to climb in).
- A clicker, if that is your chosen marker.
- Lots of tiny, high-value treats.
- A low-distraction training area.

Steps:

Place the box in your chosen training space and release the dog. Without giving him any cues, allow him to investigate. For every interaction with the box, even if that is just looking at it to start with, mark and reward. As the dog realises he can earn himself some tasty treats, he will begin to offer other behaviours. Mark and reward everything that he offers in relation to the box. Five to ten minutes is a good session length for this activity.

Troubleshooting:

If the dog seems worried about the box, any object can be used; just apply the same method.

If the dog ignores the box, try looking between the dog and the box; he will probably catch on and follow your line of vision.

If he wanders around the room ignoring the box, mark and reward for being somewhere near it, then wait until he is slightly nearer and mark and reward again. He should get the idea if the marker is well-established.

If he fixates on your hands when you are holding the food or a clicker, hide your hands behind your back. This will not only help him shift his focus, it will also build on a visual cue for the start of a free shaping session.

STAGE 4: DEVELOPING THE NOSEWORK

Goals:
- To develop the dog's search ability by relying more on the nose and less on vision.
- To work a little harder for the food.
- To build confidence.

You will need:
- High-value, smelly treats.
- An old towel.
- A low-distraction area for training (and away from other dogs, in case of resource guarding).
- A clicker, if that is your chosen marker.

Steps:
Now that your dog is confident with the scatter feeding activity, it is time to challenge him a little. Show your dog that you have food and then move away out of his sight, preventing him from following. Place the towel on the ground with the treats on top, then fold the towel in half to cover the treats. Release your dog into the training area and observe him to gauge his level of confidence when approaching the towel to look for the food.

Troubleshooting:
If he sniffs the towel and walks away, try a bit of encouragement.

If your marker is well-established at this point, mark each interaction towards the towel and reward with a treat dropped onto the towel until he shows confidence. If the opposite happens and he finds this exercise very easy, it can be made more difficult with more elaborate twists and folds in the towel, or by adding more towels.

Always monitor confidence levels at all stages to ensure enjoyment and that he will always succeed. This is another great activity to integrate into your dog's mealtimes.

STAGE 5: CONFIDENCE BUILDING WITH GAMES

Goals:
- To introduce more variety to the enrichment games in order to build determination, confidence, and problem solving.

You will need:
- Some imagination: the possibilities are endless!
- The old towel from the previous exercise.
- Dog-safe toys.
- Recycling materials such as paper, toilet roll and kitchen roll tubes, egg boxes and cardboard boxes.
- A clicker, if that is your chosen marker.
- High-value, smelly dog treats.

Steps:
Once the dog is happily and confidently engaging in the "food in a towel" game, it is time to add a bit of variety. A good starting point is to take the towel and simply place it in an open cardboard box (of a suitable size for the dog) to add another dimension to the game. Having completed the free-shaping exercise previously, the combination of the box and towel should not pose a problem to the dog but if he is phased, mark and reward each interaction with the box as before with some verbal encouragement, and take things slowly. When the dog can complete this stage happily, you might add a loosely fitting lid to the box to further develop the game. Another possibility is to add a little paper onto the top of the towel for him to rip up or just search through; there is no right or wrong way, as long as the dog is enjoying himself.

Troubleshooting:
Remember when increasing the difficulty level that it should be done gradually so as not to knock the dog's confidence. For

example: if adding paper to the towel in the box, leave the lid off to start with so that the dog isn't overwhelmed (unless he is a very confident dog and actively enjoys the challenge).

When the dog is ready to move on, you could remove the towel from the box and perhaps add food to it, with perhaps a toy or two on top for him to search through, or add a little more paper. Observe what your dog enjoys best, whether it is shredding things to find the food or just rooting around amongst things. If he particularly enjoys ripping and tearing, try securing some food into toilet roll tubes with a little paper inserted into each end to seal the tubes. These can be added to the box or they can be placed where you like. When the dog understands what to do with them, they can even be hidden for him to find and play with. Always supervise to ensure your dog's safety.

A way to develop this game would be to use your newly acquired shaping skills to teach your dog to tidy up after himself. Use a box or a laundry basket (of a suitable height) that your dog can drop the rubbish into; this makes the task of tidying up much more fun for you!

Feeding from recycling can be a great replacement for a slow feeder; for example, add kibble to an egg box instead of placing in a bowl. Leaving it open to start with will be a nice, simple way to present it to the dog, and the box can then be secured shut once he is confident.

The possibilities are endless, so take some time to find what your dog really enjoys; have fun and be creative! Start to integrate these games into everyday life for a calmer and more enriched lifestyle for both you and your dog.

STAGE 6: INTRODUCING A SCENTED ITEM AND TARGETING

Goals:
- To introduce a chosen scented item that will be used throughout search training.
- To teach the dog to target the scented item.
- Further develop the search cue introduced in Stage 1.

You will need:
- A scent that is not aversive or toxic, such as vanilla, ginger, catnip, sage or aniseed. (Ginger is an excellent choice because it can be introduced in biscuit form, boosting motivation for the dog).
- A safe fabric article such as a cloth or a sock.
- A small Tupperware box with holes in that will go inside the fabric item. This should be of a suitable size to be picked up, carried and played with by the dog.
- A low-distraction training area outdoors.
- A clicker, if that is your chosen marker.
- High-value treats.

Steps:
Place the prepared search item on the ground in front of the dog and wait for him to touch it. When he does, mark and reward.

Troubleshooting:
If he doesn't approach and touch the item, place a treat on the top of it to help him, then mark and reward after he takes the treat. Repeat this a few times and then pretend to place a treat; mark and reward as he touches it. Practise until he is confident with this step.

Repeat the process again, but this time, add your search cue as the dog touches the item, then mark and reward. Move the item to a new position, give the cue as he touches it, and then mark and reward. To strengthen this behaviour, place the item in lots of different positions and at varied heights, being careful to match the increasing difficulty level to the dog's confidence. Once this is well-established, the cue can be brought forward so that he is searching on cue (using the cue word to prompt the touch, instead of *as* he touches it).

End the session on a high, followed by playtime!

STAGE 7: TARGET TO RETRIEVE

Goals:
- To progress from targeting the item to picking it up, developing into a retrieve.

You will need:
- The scented item.
- A clicker, if that is your chosen marker.
- High-value treats.
- A low-distraction training area.

Steps:
By this point, the dog should be confident in targeting the search item. To progress to picking it up, (if the dog hasn't already done this), delay the marker to encourage him to take it.

Troubleshooting:
If the dog lacks confidence, mark and reward all the bite-sized actions that build towards picking up the item. For example: mark and reward the mouth opening, then touching the item, then teeth making contact with it, then any attempts to hold it in the mouth, and continue until the dog can pick it up and hold it comfortably.

Once the dog is picking up the item, have some fun with it. Throw it a little way for the dog to chase after and fetch, giving the search cue as you do so. Use all of your training area to throw the item in different directions, ensuring it is a fun game for the dog. Always give lots of rewards and praise to help build incentive, motivation, and excitement. Practise makes perfect!

STAGE 8: DEVELOPING THE SEARCH AND RETRIEVE SKILLS

Goals:
- To build confidence in fetching the search item from more varied areas.
- To teach the dog to search above ground level.
- To engage the dog's nose more.
- To observe the dog's indication style as he starts to search for the unseen item.

You will need:
- The scented search item.
- High-value treats.
- A clicker, if that is your chosen marker.
- A more varied outdoor training area.
- A willing assistant.

Steps:
This stage will begin as an extension of the previous one. Gradually increase the difficulty level by throwing the search item into slightly more complex areas within your training area, such as into long grass, into a bush, at different heights (providing that it is safe). Remember to use your search cue and tailor the session to your dog's confidence and ability level, always ensuring that he is having fun.

To develop this step, ask your assistant to turn your dog away as the search item lands, so that he engages his nose more when searching. Consider the wind direction at this point and how the dog will approach the search area; set him up to succeed. Finish the session on a high and with some playtime. Practise, practise,

practise to proof the scented item retrieval before moving on to the next stage. "Proofing" means practising something in lots of situations and settings so that your dog can perform it anywhere, even with distractions present.

STAGE 9: MULTI-DROPS

Goals:
- To introduce a more complex search by faking the placing of the scent item.
- To strengthen the dog's scent recognition.

You will need:
- Your scented search article.
- High-value treats.
- A clicker, if that is your chosen marker.
- A willing assistant.
- A low-distraction training area outdoors, preferably with a few trees.

Steps:
Choose an area with a vantage point for your dog and some potential hiding places that are in view, such as at the base of trees (your dog will naturally be drawn to investigate these). Ask your willing assistant to hold your dog where he can see everything and then show him the scented search item. Have a game with him and the search item to build his excitement. Next, put it out of his sight and walk or run between the hiding places while moving in one direction. Pretend to drop the search item in one or two places, then place it on the last drop. Continue moving in the same direction towards your dog, (don't go back on yourself) and then show him you no longer have the search item. Release your dog, cue him to search and then observe. He should automatically go to the last hiding place, where you placed the search item. Finding the prize on his first attempt should be a great confidence boost, so have a party with him to celebrate! If he doesn't find the search item on

his first try and chooses a different route, he should still find it fairly quickly by limiting the number of potential drops. As he becomes more confident, more hiding places can be added to increase the difficulty level, but always cater to the dog and be careful to avoid a loss of confidence.

Finish the session on a high with some playtime!

STAGE 10: INCREASING THE DIFFICULTY OF MULTI-DROP TRAINING

Goals:
- For the dog to cope with scent contamination in the fake drop places.
- To introduce more difficult hides alongside scent contamination.
You will need:
- Your scented search item.
- High-value treats.
- A clicker, if that is your chosen marker.
- A willing assistant.
- A training area outdoors, preferably with a few trees.

Steps:
Stage nine will need to have been practised lots in order to build confidence and determination, now that the dog is working harder. Once he can search an area with four or five hiding places, introduce scent contamination to the fake drops by handling the search item and then rubbing your hands and the search item around the fake drop areas. Start with contaminating only one search area to help the dog distinguish between that and the real drop, as he may struggle with the scent disturbance initially. Practise until all fake drops are contaminated, and the dog can still find the search item.

Once this is well-established, work your dog's nose a little harder still by making the search item more difficult to find. You will probably need to reduce the scent contamination while you gradually increase the difficulty of the hide, until your dog can cope with this as well as the scent contamination. Remember not to overwhelm your dog and finish each session with some fun and games!

STAGE 11: SEARCHING FOR AN ITEM WHICH HAS ALREADY BEEN PLACED

Goals:
- To be able to work in varied search areas.
- To be able to find a placed item without seeing it first.
- To develop handler skills, becoming more proactive.

You will need:
- Your scented search item.
- High-value treats.
- A clicker, if that is your chosen marker.
- A willing assistant.
- A hedge or fence line in a low-distraction outdoor area.

Steps:
Enter your chosen search area without your dog and hide the search item in a place where your dog will easily find it. Somewhere along a fence or hedge-line is ideal, as it will form a guideline for the dog to search along. Ask your assistant to bring your dog into the search area, with you standing at the search line. Approach your dog, showing him you don't have the search item (he should remember this gesture from the multi-drop stage). Release the dog and cue him to search, helping him along if necessary. Be aware of the wind direction and how it will affect the dog's approach to the hide. As he gains confidence, difficulty can be built gradually by hiding the search item in more difficult areas, such as in long grass, or you

could lodge it into a hedge (not a spiky one!).

Once the dog can complete these searches with confidence, try an easy hide in a more open area. Help your dog to search the whole area, staying behind him so as not to interfere with his search.

STAGE 12: BUILDING CAPACITY TO SEARCH

Now that your dog has acquired all of the necessary skills to enjoy a life of enrichment through scentwork, continue to develop these skills by practising regularly so that your dog can work in lots of different settings and distraction levels. Remember not to over-use your search cue; if you find yourself repeating it, then your dog has probably lost interest or some confidence, so revisit an easier task that he can easily succeed at. Remember to alternate easier and more difficult tasks while building duration and difficulty to avoid overwhelming your dog; increase search time gradually. Your role should develop beyond simply observing; your partnership and level of communication with your dog will continue to strengthen as you progress. The sky is the limit!

Trigger

IN CONCLUSION

I hope that you have found the book helpful, and a source of enjoyment and entertainment. It has given me hours of pleasure reading through emails, having a giggle at the various stories and admiring the beautiful photos (which both proved most distracting!). I've tried my best to honour every hound in accordance with the descriptions and tales I have received, and I'm very grateful to you all for your contributions. It has been lovely to commemorate your pet trailies past and present, as well as providing much-needed insight for those who might be considering their first venture into the world of Trailhounds. Hopefully, any prospective adopters will now have a clear idea of how they can go about acquiring their very own hound, the routes available to them, what it entails and what might be in store for them! Just think of the unknown pleasures yet to come: the "flip flap… flip flap… flip flap" of the bin lid being nosed open and closed repeatedly as you try to eat your breakfast in peace; the frivolity of your hound having a crafty lick of your other half's tea cup when they aren't watching, and you accidentally (on purpose) neglect to inform them. Or, you might be sitting comfortably on the sofa one minute and then find your legs being rudely pawed out of the way, followed by a bottom landing on you heavily. Then, four legs are suddenly bracing between you and the sofa to oust you from your seat and onto the floor. I recall having to attempt an imitation of Usain Bolt on the beach one day, as I spotted some horses a considerable way away. I quickly checked to make sure that the hounds were all obliviously sniffing around still, only to realise, as Jack disappeared into the distance with an accomplice, that he was sniffing the trail of hoofprints which heart-stoppingly continued across the beach, fading into the horizon towards the next town along which was five miles away; the list goes on….

When I made the decision to take on this project, it felt extremely daunting. I was concerned that I wouldn't have enough material, I wouldn't be capable of completing it, I wouldn't be able to find the time, and so on. However, once I actually started, I realised that all of the study and reading I have done since my hounds came into my life has been geared towards this book; it almost feels as though it has written itself. Having experienced some anxiety and reactivity with my own dogs, I've witnessed first-hand the lack of understanding surrounding it and how a single encounter with a member of the "my dog is friendly" brigade can upset your dog and cause him stress. Granted, some parts of the book are quite serious and there are some rather heavy topics, but they are intended only as a preventative measure and to raise awareness. I'm very passionate about being proactive in helping dogs to feel safe and secure, building confidence and resilience while learning how to read their communications and understand them on a deeper level. I'm a huge believer in addressing the emotions rather than responding purely to the external display of behaviour; it is far kinder and more ethical to help our dog to feel better about the things which worry them, rather than simply aiming for a degree of tolerance and acceptance.

We should always strive to set our dogs up for success and actively manage interactions, as well as their environment, whilst also providing them with choices. However, they are not always capable of making the right choices and may need some help along the way. Secure fields are an absolute blessing so it is well worth locating one in your area to hire for playdates, and to provide a safe place for them to blow off some steam and have a good sniff off the lead. Sniffing is hugely enjoyable and will help your hound to relax after an adrenaline-filled run-around. I have found scentwork and mantrailing to be hugely beneficial in promoting calm, building confidence and resilience, and my hounds absolutely love it! Having an outlet to use their biggest asset is vital for their health and happiness, which is why I have included my enrichment and scentwork plan. It should become a part of your daily routine and will be an enjoyable activity to do together, which will help to develop your relationship and build on your partnership.

I feel rather sad to have almost come to the end of this project. I've thoroughly enjoyed researching the sport and history of hound trailing, along with the work of the Lakeland Trailhound Welfare, and it's been absolutely fantastic to have the opportunity to ask all of the questions that have gathered in my mind over the last few years since having my own hounds, but never had the chance (or the courage) to ask. Since having our hounds, Trigger and Jack, my husband and I have returned to the Lake District each year (pre-COVID-19) and have been along to the trails, being made to feel extremely welcome by the trailing community, who have always shown an interest in our hounds. I have always wondered about the training side of things and found it fascinating that despite the hounds being so very independent, they are still capable of covering the distance and terrain that they do, without detouring from the trail (well, most do!) I also have a greater sense of the close community of people involved in trailing, both those who race them and those who adopt these wonderful hounds.

When compiling the stories, it soon became apparent how well known each and every hound is, with details provided of their date of birth, their dam and sire, other siblings, why they were retired and how, and so on. I have also come to realise how many adopters remain in contact with their hound's racing family, and how many friendships have blossomed through the sport of trailing. The hound trailing community are truly remarkable people who are hugely dedicated to their hounds, as well as to the sport. It feels rather like a secret society, combined with a large, supportive and wonderful family which only the luckiest of people have the chance to venture into. For the uninitiated amongst you, what an adventure you are yet to have!

Hannah Baron's Cody Lad

BIBLIOGRAPHY

Hound Trailing: A history of the Sport in Cumbria, by John Coughlan. Published by the author, first edition 1998.

Hounds: Hunting By Scent, by David Hancock. Published by The Crowood Press Ltd, first edition 27th January 2014.

Mission Possible: Positive Canine Coaching and Enrichment Through Scentwork Books 1 & 2, by Sally Gutteridge. Published independently, 18th November 2018.

When Pigs Fly! Training Success With Impossible Dogs, by Jane Killion. Published by Dogwise Publishing, (illustrated edition) 22nd June 2007.

Fight or Fright? A Reactive Dog Guardian's Handbook, by Jay Gurden. Published independently, 25th January 2019.

Understanding Reactive Dogs: Why Dogs React and How to Help, by Jay Gurden. Published independently, 8th January 2021.

Canine Confidence, Your End of the Lead: Changing How You Think and Act To Help Your Reactive Dog, by Janet Finlay. Published independently, 3rd June 2019.

Inspiring Resilience in Fearful and Reactive Dogs, by Sally Gutteridge. Published independently, 20th October 2018.

Lessons From Your Reactive Dog, by Sally Gutteridge. Published independently, 20th August 2019.

Canine Communication: The Language of a Species, by Sally Gutteridge. Published independently, 18th January 2019.

On Talking Terms With Dogs: Calming Signals, by Turid Rugaas. Published by Dogwise Publishing, 2nd edition 1st January 2006.

Be Right Back! How To Overcome Your Dog's Separation Anxiety And Regain Your Freedom, by Julie Naismith. Published by Pitmore Publishing, 22nd November 2019.

REFERENCES

Various issues of the London Gazette, individually referenced within the text.

https://en.m.wikipedia.org/wiki/Hound_trailing

http://lakelandhuntingmemories.com/TrailsNew.html
Hound Trailing, by Margaret Baxter, of the Hound Trailing Association. Site created 20th April 2008, © Cumbrian Lad 2008-2017. All rights reserved.

http://www.trailhoundwelfare.org.uk/
© Lakeland Trailhound Welfare 2015. All rights reserved.

https://www.houndtrailing.org.uk
© HTA Ltd.

https://borderhoundtrailing.co.uk

https://www.frontiersin.org/articles/10.3389/fvets.2020.00388/full
Frontiers in Veterinary Science: Animal Reproduction-Theriogenology. This article is part of the research topic "Effective Options Regarding Spay or Neuter of Dogs".
Original research article Front. Vet. Sci., 7th July 2020. https://doi.org/10.3389/fvets.2020.00388.

http://www.southerncharmlabradoodles.com/downloads/spay-_neuter_considerations_2013.pdf
Early Spay-Neuter Considerations for the Canine Athlete: One Veterinarian's Opinion. © 2005 Chris Zink DVM, PhD, DACVP, DACVSMR. Extensively revised and updated 2013. Canine Sports Productions- www.caninesports.com.

https://www.animaltrainingacademy.com/how-to-animal-training/training-plans/
Animal Training Academy: Lesson 5- How to Write Animal Training Plans.
© 2021 Animal Training Academy.

https://www.dogtrainingplanner.co.uk/how-to-write-a-dog-training-plan/
How to Write a Dog Training Plan: 3 Easy Steps, by George Watts. 3rd April 2016, Dog Training Tips.

https://www.clickertraining.com/node/2090
Karen Pryor Clicker Training. How to Write a Training Plan-Part One, by trainer@canines…, 1st January 2009. Filed in "Skills for Every Day".

https://animalwellnessmagazine.com/reactive-vs-aggressive-dogs/?amp
Animal Wellness. Reactive vs. Aggressive Dogs, by Marybeth Bittel, 25th July 2017.

https://www.dogster.com/lifestyle/is-your-dog-reactive-or-aggressive-how-to-tell-the-difference-and-what-to-do
Dogster. Is Your Dog Reactive or Aggressive? How to Tell the Difference and What to Do, by dogedit, 24th February 2017. © 2021, Belvoir Media Group. All rights reserved.

https://www.whole-dog-journal.com/behavior/causes-of-reactive-dog-behavior-and-how-to-train-accordingly/
Whole Dog Journal. Causes of Reactive Dog Behavior and How to Train Accordingly: Dealing with dogs who "go off" or "lose it" in certain circumstances, by Pat Miller, CBCC-KA, CPDT-KA. Published 10th October 2003.

https://www.sciencedirect.com/science/article/abs/pii/S1558787815001975
Science Direct: Journal of Veterinary Behavior, volume 11, January-February 2016, pages 13-17.
Research: Owner-reported aggressive behavior towards familiar people may be a more prominent occurrence in pet shop-traded dogs. Federica Pirrone, Ludovica Pierantoni, Giovanni Quintavalle Pastorino, Mariangela Albertini. *Department of Veterinary Science and Public Health, University of Milan, Milan, Italy. *CAN (Comportamento Animale Napoli), Naples, Italy. Received 23rd June 2015, revised 13th November 2015, accepted 25th November 2015, available online 8th December 2015. © 2016, Elsevier Inc. All rights reserved.
https://doi.org/10.1016/j.jveb.2015.11.007

https://www.akc.org/expert-advice/training/reactivity-vs-aggression/
American Kennel Club. What Is Aggression? Dog Reactivity vs. Dog Aggression, by Erin Rakosky, DVM. August 19th, 2020. © The American Kennel Club, Inc. 2021. All rights reserved.

https://www.whole-dog-journal.com/health/the-canine-sense-of-smell/
Whole Dog Journal. The Canine Sense of Smell: Sniffing out the source of our dogs' remarkable ability to smell, by Randy Kidd. Published 14th October 2004, updated 23rd April 2019. © Belvoir Media Group, LLC. All rights reserved.

https://www.nomnomnow.com/learn/article/understanding-a-dogs-sense-of-smell
Learn: Puppy Care, Understanding A Dog's Sense of Smell. © 2021 NomNomNow Inc.

https://theanimalrescuesite.greatergood.com
The Animal Rescue Site. Copyright 2000-2021 The Animal Rescue Site and GreaterGood. All rights reserved. Owned and operated by CharityUSA.com, LLC.

https://www.petsforpatriots.org/partner-news/impacts-of-long-term-sheltering-dogs/
Pets For Patriots, Partner News. Impacts Of long-term sheltering on dogs. 24th October 2017. © 2021 Pets for Patriots, Inc.

https:/pflugervillepetsalive.org/the-effects-of-an-animal-shelter-on-a-dog/
Pflugerville Pets Alive! The Effects of An Animal Shelter On A Dog, by WebAdmin, 20th January 2016. © 2020 Pflugerville Pets Alive. All rights reserved.

https://youtu.be/FKjNzZmZ5fk
Dogkind: Training sensitive dogs to love their harness (part 1)
https://youtu.be/ij8HCdNQ3ek
Dogkind: Training sensitive dogs to love their harness (part 2)

https://www.companionanimalpsychology.com/2016/12/how-to-choose-dog-trainer.html
Companion Animal Psychology. How to Choose a Dog Trainer: How to choose the best dog trainer for you and your dog, including the methods and qualifications to look for, by Zazie Todd, PhD, 14th December 2016.

https://moderndogmagazine.com/articles/which-emotions-do-dogs-actually-experience/32883
Modern Dog: the lifestyle magazine for modern dogs and their companions. Which Emotions Do Dogs Actually Experience? Do Dogs Have Feelings? The feelings dogs actually experience-and those we project, by Stanley Coren. Illustration by Kim Smith.

https://www.culturedcanine.co.uk/post/should-i-use-a-harness
Cultured Canine Dog Training: Dog Training and Behaviour Modification in Hambleton and York. Should I Use a Harness? By Holly Adgo, 1st October 2018.

https://www.legislation.gov.uk/uksi/1992/901/made
legislation.gov.uk: The Control of Dogs Order 1992.
© Crown and database right.

https://www.ntu.ac.uk/about-us/news/news-articles/2020/05/collars-risk-causing-neck-injuries-in-dogs,-study-shows
Nottingham Trent University. Collars risk causing neck injuries in dogs, study shows. Collars risk causing neck injuries in dogs as they pull on the lead or the lead is jerked by the owner, new research suggests. Published 4th May 2020. © Nottingham Trent University.

https://stneotspetcare.co.uk/2020/12/06/collar-or-harness/?fbclid=IwAR1o2u5fHW
St Neots Pet Care: Caring for your pets. Collar or Harness?

https://www.sciencedaily.com/releases/2018/03/180320100719.htm
Science Daily: Science News. Dogs with noise sensitivity should be routinely assessed for pain by vets. University of Lincoln, 20th March 2018.

https://www.whole-dog-journal.com/health/pains-effect-on-behavior/

Whole Dog Journal: Pain's Effect on Behavior, by Jessica Hekman. Published 23rd March 2020, updated 30th June 2020. © Belvoir Media Group, LLC. All rights reserved.

www.canineprinciples.com

ABOUT THE AUTHOR

Emily lives on a farm estate in rural Norfolk with her husband
David and Trailhounds Trigger and Jack. Emily is very passionate
about her hounds and has a great interest in canine behaviour, with
a particular soft spot for nervous dogs. In June 2020, Emily joined
the admin team of a Facebook group which provides training
advice, help and guidance to guardians of fearful, anxious and
reactive dogs. The group has a strict ethos supporting force-free

and science-based Best Practice, with a narrow focus on management, positive reinforcement, counterconditioning and desensitisation. Emily has also recently become a moderator for a second Facebook group, which specialises in shy and fearful dogs. In addition, Emily has been asked to join a team of dedicated professionals to create an online advice and support group which will provide educational resources for rescue dog guardians and fosterers. The group will also liaise with rescue shelters to provide guidance and will help them fully transition to force free handling and training methods; a really exciting project to be involved with!

Emily dedicates a great deal of time to reading and learning, and studies continuously, amassing an extensive collection of books and many completed courses along the way. Emily qualified as a Canine Body Language Specialist with the Dog Training College, and from Canine Principles, she holds accredited certificates in Scentwork Enrichment and Canine Anxiety, as well as accredited advanced certificates in Canine Reactive Behaviour and Rescue Dogs. It was the wonderful courses of Canine Principles which led to her contemplating the writing and completion of this book, having received their thirty-day book writing course as a Christmas present. A new writing course has recently been launched, which Emily is very much looking forward to pursuing.

Emily and Jack enjoy Scentwork UK and Mantrailing UK lessons together, and will soon be turning a paw to tracking, as well. They have found both activities to be extremely valuable learning experiences, and a great way to develop their relationship, whilst extending their skills and building Jack's confidence. Highly recommended and lots of fun!

In 2015, Emily created the *Norfolk Unofficial Trailhounds Group* Facebook page in order to connect hound guardians and to share photographs and stories, while also providing a point of contact to arrange local get-togethers. Please feel free to use the page to share news and get in touch; Emily can also be contacted via email: emilysavage80@gmail.com, and would love to hear from you!

INDEX